S0-DUS-264

The Business of Horses
Creating A Successful Horse Business
Second Edition

M. R. Bain

outskirtspress
DENVER, COLORADO

The opinions expressed in this manuscript are solely the opinions of the author and do not represent the opinions or thoughts of the publisher. The author has represented and warranted full ownership and/or legal right to publish all the materials in this book.

The Business of Horses
Creating A Successful Horse Business Second Edition
All Rights Reserved.
Copyright © 2014 M. R. Bain
v2.0

Cover Photo © 2014 M.R. Bain. All rights reserved - used with permission.

This book may not be reproduced, transmitted, or stored in whole or in part by any means, including graphic, electronic, or mechanical without the express written consent of the publisher except in the case of brief quotations embodied in critical articles and reviews.

Outskirts Press, Inc.
http://www.outskirtspress.com

ISBN: 978-1-4787-2198-7

Outskirts Press and the "OP" logo are trademarks belonging to Outskirts Press, Inc.

PRINTED IN THE UNITED STATES OF AMERICA

Dedication

Thanks to MaryAnn for giving me a reason to continue and to June for standing by with encouragement when I needed it most.

Table of Contents

Foreword

Note; There have been so many changes to the business of horses since 2007 that I thought it would be prudent to include them in a revised edition. Also, some of you have wanted greater detail of some of the items in the first book. I will endeavor to explain them in this book.

There are now many more obstacles for us, as horse people, to contend with including certain groups and government agencies that are limiting our marketing efforts and how we can govern the supply of unwanted animals.

We must be aware of the changes made by our elected officials to the way we do business. They will definitely affect the way we conduct our affairs.

Many of us have a love affair with the horse and so we buy a horse. We board it at a stable and have it trained and maybe show it. If it is a mare, sooner or later, we will want to breed it and raise a foal. Eventually, we start looking for our own place to buy or rent, so we can keep our horse costs down. And then we start boarding or training other people's horses and we are in the horse business. And as we enter the world of horses, how we set up our business entity and how we conduct that business will determine whether we are successful or not.

I remember why I got into the horse business. I liked working with horses; in fact I would do that instead of eating, sleeping or looking at girls. My parents were sure that their oldest son was going to work in the corporate structure and let someone else sign the checks. They held the view that the day of the horse had come and gone, that the age of mechanization was here and that horses were now a hobby afforded by those with disposable income. This view is still held today by many including the IRS. Yet, in this age of technology, we have more horses and people involved with them than we have had in the last 60 years. While we do not use them for transportation or as beasts of burden, we continue to use them for recreation and on large ranches. When I started, I was naive enough to believe that I could make a living at doing what I love, training horses. I know now that it can be done and over the years I have learned that the secret is to treat it as a job, not as a hobby or something that I like to do. You learn that in order to make the payments on the mortgage, the truck, and buy food for the children that you must get up in the morning and sell your inventory or services. You must always be aware of changes in the marketplace and strive to incorporate them in to your business or to make your products and services more needed.

How do you convince the skeptics that you are in business to make money, acquire assets, that you have inventory that has value and that you are not listed on the Forbes 500? You must treat it like a business rather than as something that you would do for free. Often, we fail do to that because we fall in love with a certain breed, certain color, certain horse, etc. Don't! We should conduct our activities as if our livelihood depends on it. It does! If we want to be in business and show that our intent is to provide ourselves with an income that we can depend on over a period of time, we must be ready to part with our inventory at a fair price in a reasonable length of time.

We should, at some time, be able to depend on our business to provide us with a suitable income that would compare to income earned in other employment (IRS auditors look for this.) Many times horse business owners have income from other employment that provides them with substantial resources that can be used in starting up and maintaining a horse business. The problem is that the owner does not keep a record of the amount of money invested in the business nor has proof (signed financial documents) that the investment is to be repaid at some period, either during the life of the business or at the close of the business.

We devote large amounts of time to our horses. If we are in business, we must devote large amounts of time to it. Did I repeat myself? No! The business owner has to devote time to selling his product, adjusting his inventory, researching market conditions, looking for new customers for his product, teaching new and old employees and a myriad of other duties.

All businesses in the start-up phase have cash flow problems. Namely, no cash flow. That is normal. Most horse businesses have little capital to start with, just a dream and a lot of ambition. The entrepreneurial owner learns early on to read each little change and to act quickly on it. What is hot now is history tomorrow. That is true in the horse industry especially where today's hot bloodlines or breeds change at the next world show or GR1 race. You have to be willing to change, to add new blood to your breeding programs, to offer lessons in disciplines that are developing increasing interest in your area, to train a different type of horse in order to increase your cash flow and improve your profitability.

We should have goals—attainable goals. We should learn from others who are successful but we should also be innovative in our approach to setting up a business in our particular area. The goals should be attainable in a reasonable length of time. If your losses are reduced over time and your income increases in the same period, you know that you are doing something right and your business can become successful. If your losses continue to increase and you are putting large amounts of money into the business, you need to either revise your business plan or decide if you are a hobbyist. Do not wait for the bank or IRS to make that decision, you won't like the outcome.

All too often, we either develop tunnel vision or we use a shotgun approach. We think that if someone does it a certain way then it will work for us. Or we want to leave nothing uncovered so we have a little bit of everything without a definite plan of action or research into the opportunities that may be present. Every business can carve out its own niche in the business world by being innovative and aware of the customer's needs and serving those needs. A business should always be looking for new ways to serve its clientele and for securing new customers.

Our greatest adversary is not the person down the street but ourselves. Many of our financial problems stem from trying to beat the competition on price when it is far more important to provide unbeatable service to our customers and meet the wants and needs of that clientele. It is not the storefront but the people in the store that brings repeat and new customers and keeps a business growing and prospering.

According to a survey conducted in 2005 for The American Horse Council, the horse industry involves 4.6 million owners, service providers, employees and volunteers and 9.2 million horses. The industry produces goods and services of $39 billion and has a total impact on the gross domestic product (GDP) of $102 billion.

It employs 701,946 people and generates 1.4 million full-time equivalent jobs in related employment across the U.S. More people are directly employed by the horse industry than in railroads, radio and television broadcasting, petroleum and coal products manufacturing and tobacco product manufacturing.

The business is highly diverse supporting a variety of activities throughout the country. It combines the rural activities of breeding, training, maintaining and riding horses with the urban activities of operating racetracks, horse shows and public stables.

The median income for horse-owning households is $60,000. The industry can and does provide jobs for people with meaningful income whether they are owners or employees. If your love is the horse and you enjoy working with people from a multitude of backgrounds whose interests are the same as yours, then maybe you should consider a business involving horses.

You do not have to be a trainer or own a facility to be involved in this horse business world. There are many careers available that allow you to make a living wage and be deeply involved in the industry. I know that most of you reading this want to have your own facility that will do multiple endeavors with horses but before that can happen, you must learn what to do and when to do it.

In the following pages, I will share with you my opinions and experiences on how to set up your horse business and maintain it in a profitable manner with as few headaches as possible and as much fun as possible. Whether your goal is to ride the next world champion, produce that champion or just help other people to do that, we must have a plan of action. This should be used as a road map to guide you to your goals and help you in attaining them.

1

Planning For Success

When a person decides to start a business, often they look at what other people are doing and which ones seem to be successful. They may not have any idea whether it has many stockholders or just one, is a corporation, partnership or sole proprietorship or whether it is really successful or an interesting sideline for someone's disposal income. The new entrepreneur may decide to do many things at once and therefore make lots of money or lose lots of money. No matter if you use a shotgun approach or not, the first place to start is a business plan. A business plan will give you a guideline to follow and can predict whether you will be successful or not. It is much less costly to fail on paper than after you have invested time and money in the project.

Planning is the key to a successful business of any sort. A business plan is a simple tool that provides you, your banker, your accountant, attorney and the IRS with a roadmap of how you are going to accomplish your goals. It will provide a way of determining when you should change your product mix, alter the way you are going or if you need to reevaluate your goals.

A business plan can be a few sentences about who you are, your expertise, education, investment, goals, market surveys or it can be more detailed. In my opinion, the more detail the better. It gives you time to think, to ask others in the industry about their experiences. It provides us with the opportunity to research what is happening in the rest of the world and what might be needed or desired by customers in our area.

First, you want to describe your facility or farm and how it will be used in the business. If you are into horses, the barn, fences, land and location come first. The house is where you go when there is nothing else to do, which is seldom. Too often people buy the house and then decide to have a horse business. A horse business is like any other business—location, location, location. Your facility should be easily accessible to the potential customer. If they have to drive miles back in the woods in order to reach you, they will probably only visit you once. True, it may be your dream but remember this. Wal-Mart succeeded by building stores that were readily accessible to a large number of people living in rural areas

Second, give a summary of the industry using the AHC survey and how your business will fill a need in your area or region or nationally that is being underserved. There may be a need for better horses, stables, and trainers, whatever. If you are a breeder, a particular bloodline or price range may be needed. By doing the research that is necessary to arrive at an informed decision, you will have a better idea of what is going on in your area. You could conduct a survey of the local area participants and their wants and needs. Or, you could ask the public for input as to what they want. It could be a horse rental, a place for abandoned horses or a retirement facility for older horses. You will not find out unless you ask questions and follow the results. Much too often, we fail to do this vital research and as a consequence, we have to abandon our endeavor before it has a chance to succeed.

Third, give a background on yourself, your employees, and whoever else is actively involved in your business i.e. outside trainers or instructors. Tell about everyone's education and what they have done, emphasizing any outstanding accomplishments. List all clinics or classes that have been taken in order to further your knowledge of the industry and business, any certifications and degrees that have been awarded you or the other people involved. Include a list of your inventory of horses, equipment, facilities, etc. Why each is unique to the area being served. This one area where you need to take time and explain in detail how and what each item is going to be used.

Fourth, the most thought provoking task. How are you going to sell your product and when? To put this in perspective if you owned a store and the inventory did not sell, you would mark it down and replace it with something that would sell readily. You would advertise on a consistent basis so everyone would know where to get it when they wanted it. That is what you have to do if you have a horse business of any kind. Whether you are a tack store, breeding farm, boarding stable or trainer, your product or service has to be something that customers want and need. A well thought out marketing plan will help you do this.

Fifth, everyone, you, your banker, your accountant and your attorney will want to know what it going to cost for this business. It costs money to acquire facilities, (whether you lease or buy), inventory, expenses to maintain the business during the startup phase. If the costs exceed the expected income after a reasonable time, only you will know the answer and the IRS would like to hear it to add to its list. Be conservative in

estimating income and exaggerate your costs and maybe everyone including you will be pleasantly surprised. Startup businesses need time to gain a foothold in the marketplace. You
can not accomplish your goals overnight in most cases but only
after a lot of time, effort and money have been invested. Be
conservative, a new barn and house comes at the end of the
road. What goes on in reaching that point is more important.
You can expect highs and lows because that is life.

What a Business Plan Should Include

1. Description and History of participants and horse
   facility
   a. Who you are and what your experience is.
   b. How your facility is unique and designed for the
      market.

2. Summary of the Horse industry
   a. The American Horse Council 2005 survey is a
      good place to start.
   b. How your particular talents and farm or facility fit
      in the area that you are doing business.

3. Goals
   a. What you want to accomplish
   b. Establish a time line of what and when events will
      occur

4. Background of all participants
   a. Have you been successful in other businesses?
   b. What have you done?

5. Education and who you have consulted with (board of advisors)
   a. College? School of hard knocks? Equine courses?
   b. Have you talked to others in the industry? An attorney? An accountant? Your bank?

6. Inventory
   a. Horses, truck, trailer, tack

7. Marketing plan
   a. Showing or racing plan
      1. What are you going to do to achieve your goals?
   b. Results of plan
      1. Based on what has happened in the past and what is expected to happen in the future
   c. Advertising
      1. Develop an advertising plan.
      2. Tell how it helps you gain name recognition and be able to market your product efficiently and for a profit.

8. Costs of the horse program
   a. What it will cost for the first year
   b. What is will cost after that

9. When you can expect a profit (best guess) based on similar enterprises.
   a. This is what the IRS and your bank wants to know.

It is extremely important that your business plan be as detailed as you can make it. If it happens that you are audited by the IRS, a business plan that is up to date can help prove your case that you are a business. Horse businesses are extremely susceptible to an audit because in most cases the owner has a primary income from other sources not related to horses. If that is your case and your business is just one of your sources of income, be sure that you put in a reasonable amount of hours attending to that business. Consult with your accountant as to how many hours are required for your particular business by the IRS and keep a journal of those hours devoted to your horse enterprise. As previously stated, the business plan is your road map of how you are going to accomplish your goals. Review it on a regular basis and make changes to it as needed.

2

Structuring Your Business

There are four different ways that we can own our business; sole proprietorship, partnerships, corporations and limited liability corporations. We can change the way we do business as it grows. We can go from a sole proprietorship to a partnership to an S corporation or Limited Liability Corporation or back to a simpler form. However, the most important thing is to limit the liability to our personal assets.

Sole proprietorship means that you own your business. It is the form that most horse people start with. It is simple to set-up and to use for first-time entrepreneurs and the easiest to get out of if things don't go right. It has one owner who pays income tax and deducts losses on his personal return. You will have to pay self-employment taxes on the income received. You will have unlimited liability for all debts, lawsuits that may occur and anything else that affects the business. Your personal assets are at risk in most cases for the simple reason that everything is under your name. That is one reason why you may want to choose another type of business entity if you are worried about losing any of your personal assets.

Partnerships are of two types. A general partnership has 2 or more partners who share profits, losses, taxes and liability. Each partner is responsible for everything that the other partners do and is liable for the actions of the other partners. Limited partnerships have a managing partner who makes the decisions for the rest of the partners and is responsible to them. The partners share in the costs, losses, profits and the liability unless the partnership agreement says otherwise.

Syndicates are an example of a limited partnership. Partners buy shares or breeding rights of the syndicated horse. The managing partner is the partner who may own more shares than the rest of the partners or is the original owner, who decided to limit his liability and expenses by doing a partnership. The rest of the partners pay their share of the expenses and in return receive a share of the profits or breeding rights.

A word of caution. If you do not trust your partners implicitly, a partnership may not be for you. Profits and losses flow through to the partners and are reported on their personal income tax returns. A written partnership agreement is a must, detailing everything that you may encounter in the course of the partnership. It should include who makes the decisions for the partnership, what each partner is responsible for, how each partner pays their share of the costs and how profits are distributed and when.

The next form of ownership is the corporation. It offers liability protection to its shareholders, pays tax on the profits, has 100% deductible health insurance for employees/shareholders, fringe benefits plans for employees/shareholders, profits are taxed at 15% if retained by corporation instead of your higher personal rate. Losses are not deducible on your personal tax return and dividends are taxed again at the personal level.

Another form of the corporation is the S corporation. The

S corporation offers liability protection; profits and losses flow through to the shareholder and are reported on personal tax returns. Maximum owners allowed are 100 but it can be one person or a family.

The fact that you can protect your personal assets from liability of the business is of utmost importance. You should have separate accounts for your personal and business activities in order to maintain limited liability and provide the IRS with less ammunition if they were to audit you. The S corporation does not protect you against liability for your own actions. The S Corporation has to file a tax return even if it does not in itself pay taxes. The state in which you do business may also want a return, check with your accountant.

You may be an employee as well as an owner of an S corporation. The corporation may pay FICA taxes and the employee and employer would be subject to normal employment taxes. Pay yourself the going wage for employment unless you really like to talk to the IRS auditors. While the corporation can pay benefits such as health and accident insurance, if you own more than 2% of the S corporation, that amount is added back to your gross income and you will pay regular income tax on it.

Other things to consider. You are allowed only one class of stock, all stockholders of the corporation must agree to the S corporation. And all profits and losses are passed through proportionately to the shareholder's stake in the company. An S corporation may have only one stockholder which is also the owner. The owner may be the president and treasurer or secretary of the corporation.

In my experience, an S corporation is desirable for several reasons. It protects your personal assets (house, personal belongings, personal checking account, and car) from being seized to pay claims against the company. If your business has a great deal of liability, and what horse business doesn't, you could be sued and lose everything.

As our business progresses, we acquire assets needed to run or improve that business, such as land, buildings, trucks, trailers, livestock, houses for employees and ourselves. The problem now becomes how to shelter those assets from being subject to the liability from our business.

One of the ways of doing this is for us to have two separate business entities. One owns the property and the other rents the facility and conducts the business. You can own the land, buildings and house as a landlord and rent the barns and land to your horse business, which is a separate business. My suggestion would be for the company to rent or lease the facilities and the farm to be owned as a personal asset. You can have the corporation own the farm and rent the facility and house back to the business.

As a landlord, you can collect rent and still depreciate the buildings. You can expense the upkeep to the buildings. Your house is your home and should be treated as such. If you have employee housing on the grounds, you should collect rent from the tenants or the business if housing is part of the employee's benefits.

You have effectively limited your liability to the assets of the business and have protected in part your other assets. You can have both entities be a corporation but when you sell the farm you will pay taxes on your home because it is part of a business and not a private residence.

If you are a corporation, the business can go on if something happens to one of the shareholders. It is one of the ways you can pass the business on to other family members or you can sell just the business and retain your personal assets.

A Limited Liability Corporation are similar to an S

Corporation but at the individual state level instead of the Federal. They cost less than an S corporation to set up and are easier to understand. They do offer liability protection, can be one person or many, (there is no maximum), profits and losses are passed through to personal returns. BUT owners get taxed with self-employment tax same as partnerships and sole proprietorships. They are not available in all states and differ from state to state in how they are taxed. If you are considering this as alternative to the S corp., you should consult with your attorney and accountant before doing so. Ask questions and be fully informed.

You may want to finance the purchase of horses and other equipment by getting a loan on the horses and other assets that the business has. There are very few investors available that will advance funds without some sort of collateral. You should look into all the ways that are available to you and make your decision on whether you may lose all of your assets if the business does not succeed. Shelter as many of your assets as you can at all times. Because of the fluctuations in value of horses plus the fact that many bankers do not understand the horse industry; banks may want you to guarantee loans for your business by you signing as a personal guarantor. When this happens you need to know that you have just signed over your other assets, home, land and buildings to secure your loan for your business. It is imperative that the business creates its own credit history and operates as a stand alone entity. The president or managing partner and treasurer can sign for the corporation or partnership. In that way, the other participants can limit their personal liability for a negative credit rating affecting their personal credit rating.

There is one entity that is overlooked by many. A not-for-profit corporation can deduct all its expenses and depreciate everything that a for-profit can but it can not give its shareholders a part of the profit derived from the venture. Those profits have to be invested back into the company in some manner such as new structures, fences, new vehicles used by the business, salary increases, etc. A non-profit can buy and sell horses, give lessons, train horses for resale. Basically all the things, a for-profit can do.

It can apply for grants that are available for programs such as handicapped riders, wild horses and solicit funds from the public. It enjoys a tax exemption and as such is sometimes very appealing to persons running a business that is in the minority or will have a low profit margin. A non-profit should be set up by a tax professional so that everything is covered. Your tax exemption can be denied or rescinded if you do not follow the rules. If you are considering a business involving the disabled or reclaiming abused and/or aged horses, you might want to explore this avenue. Before starting such a business, you need to consult with someone who is very familiar with that type of entity.

A suggested list of things to do at the start of a business is the following. Your accountant and attorney may suggest more items that they would like for you to do.

1. Get an EIN (Employer Identification Number). It is free from the IRS and you should use it from now on. Especially if you have employees and have to withhold FICA and other employee taxes, both Federal and State. It will also provide an identity for the business separate from your personal SSN.

2. Register your business name with the state even if you are a sole proprietorship. This is required by most states and it protects your business name from being used by

someone else.

3. Create a business plan. Do your research. Remember this is how you are going to make a living in the horse industry. At this time, it is a good idea to determine your business structure and get it set up.

4. Open a separate bank account for the business. Do not mingle your personal and business expenses. Keep it well funded. You can transfer money from your personal account to the business account. On the profit and loss statements, it will show as owner equity. That is something you want to do, have equity in your business. It will help you down the road when you sell or transfer the business to another person.

5. At all times, operate under your business name. You can be a sole proprietorship, partnership, corporation, S Corporation or LLC but you should have your business name on all the contracts, leases, etc. that you use in the course of everyday business transactions.

6. File quarterly and annual reports as required by the IRS and the state in which you do business.

7. If you are a partnership, corporation or LLC, you should have an annual stockholders meeting, even if you are the only member of the organization. S corporations can have one person who is the president, treasurer and secretary. Keep a record of the minutes and records. You will need them if you are the subject of an audit.

8. Sign all documents with the business name, your name and title.

9. Procure all necessary licenses. Check with the state, county and city as to what types of licenses are required. While you are doing this, also check on any

restrictions that may apply to your business. While we usually think of a horse business as being a rural activity, we may be surrounded by urban and suburban developments which will impact our activity. You may have DEQ and ADA issues to deal with. Be prepared before you start the business and there will be no unpleasant surprises.

10. Create your board of advisors. Get an accountant (CPA preferred), an attorney who deals in business law, a bank officer who is willing to give advice, a veterinarian who specializes in equine medicine and an insurance agent who is well versed in equine insurance practices in your area.

11. Create your marketing plan. Find out what is needed in your area. Define who your potential customers are and what their needs are. Get a cost estimate the upcoming year and draw up a budget for that expenditure.

12. Do not be afraid to create a paper trail of everything you do. It may just prevent a lawsuit or unfavorable IRS audit. Proper documentation of our actions is the one thing that many of us overlook or are hesitant about doing.

3

Expenses, Depreciation, Appreciation

Being a business as opposed to a not-for-profit has many benefits when it comes to what you can expense or depreciate. What you expense or depreciate has a direct effect on your bottom line. If you are in business it can mean the difference between a profit and a loss at the end of the year. And that is important when you are trying to satisfy the IRS or your banker. You may not have more money in your pocket but on paper you will look good.

If you are a hobbyist and you sell a horse at a profit, you can report the sale and expenses (up to the sale price) on your tax return. If you are a business, you can report expenses, depreciation, and the profit or loss on your tax return. Being a business offers an opportunity that would not be available if you were a hobbyist.

Expenses are those items associated with the normal and necessary costs that are deemed conventional in having a horse business. These include; rent for the facility, electricity, feed, bedding, insurance, fuel, employee taxes paid by you, vet and vet supplies, horseshoer, show fees, membership fees, magazines related to the industry, postage, printer cartridges, office supplies, repairs to property and equipment and clothing unsuitable for other purposes. Some of you may dispute the last item but I have yet to see anyone go to work or attend a social function in their show clothes and they are a necessary item in the show ring.

Depreciation is an expense item that is a credit that is subtracted from the gross expenses and effectively increases your bottom line. If you sell the depreciated item for more than the depreciated value, you have to recover the depreciation. What you do is add the depreciation back to the sell price and that is the true selling price of the item and that is the amount that is taxable. That does not mean that the item, whether it is a horse or a farm, cannot increase in value. If you were to buy a pleasure prospect, train it, show in futurities and classes and then sell it for more than you paid for it you can still depreciate it during the time you own it. When you sell it, you would have to factor in the depreciation that you have written off when filing your tax return. Horse farms can appreciate in value, as land becomes less available for the population to build on or you significantly improve the facility. Consult your accountant about this whenever you sell a depreciated item in order to satisfy the IRS.

You can depreciate anything which has a life expectancy of three years or greater and costs over $500(some CPA's say $1000). Expense those items under $500 and with a short life expectancy.

I am of the opinion that if you are involved breeding, training or boarding horses that you should be a business. That does not mean that you can't have a not-for-profit business such as training horses in your spare time, boarding horses in your empty stalls, or breeding mares or stallions each year. But if you have a not-for-profit business, you may not be able to take all the expenses you have incurred off your gross income. There are so many more things that a for-profit business can expense or deduct, that you can't if you are a not-for-profit, such as mileage, clinics, truck, horses, equipment, barn, bad debts and the list goes on and on. The term not-for-profit that I use here should not be confused with a non-profit entity. A not-for-profit would be a hobbyist or a person who works with horses in addition to his regular employment.

According to IRS guidelines, if you are a not-for-profit, you may take deductions in the following order but only to the extent stated and if you itemize them on Schedule A.

1. Deductions you can take for personal as well as for business activities are allowed in full. In this category are home mortgage interest, taxes, and casualty losses.
2. Deductions that do not result in an adjustment to the basis of property but only to the extent your gross income from the business activity is greater than the deduction you take or could take. These include are advertising, utilities, insurance premiums, interest, etc.
3. Last are business deductions that decrease the basis of property but only to the extent that your gross income is more than you have used in the first two categories. In this area are deprecation, amortization, etc.

You can not use losses from a not-for-profit activity to off-set other income. And to be on the fair side, you must report all income on your 1040.

If you operate your business as a for-profit entity, you can do much more to preserve your assets. You can take depreciation, ordinary and necessary expenses of your business, amortize your start-up costs or if you buy an existing business, you can amortize the blue sky (goodwill, customer base, etc.) that was included.

If your attempt to go into business is unsuccessful and you are a not-for-profit entity, your costs you had before making a decision to start a specific business is nondeductible. The costs you had in beginning a new business are treated as capital expenses and you can deduct them as capital losses.

If you are a corporation and your attempts to start a new business fail, you may be able to deduct all costs associated with start-up as a loss. These include research into the business you are starting, marketing, employee's wages, etc.

You are allowed to deduct all expenses that are common and accepted for your business. You may, also, deduct expenses that are helpful and appropriate for your business. An expense does not have to be indispensable to be considered necessary to your business.

You must capitalize rather than deduct some costs. These costs are part of your initial investment in your business. There are three types of costs that you capitalize: 1. Going into business, 2. Business assets, and 3. Improvements to an asset.

The cost of any asset (land, buildings, trucks, trailers, machinery) is a capital expense. The costs of making improvements to an asset are capital expenses if they add value to the asset. If you repair an asset to prevent further deterioration that is a deductible expense that can be taken in the year the repair was done.

You cannot generally take a current deduction for a capital expense. You may take deductions for the amount you spend through depreciation, amortization or depletion. In doing so, you are able to deduct part of your cost each year over a period of years recovering your capital expense. Capital expenses are recovered by using the straight-line method (same amount is used each year) over 60 months. This is not the same as MARCS system that we use to depreciate items that we have mentioned before. In MARCS, the item is depreciated rapidly in the first few years and then more slowly over the rest of the useful life of the item. Using MARCS, allows you to recover your cost more quickly because it assumes that the asset depreciates more rapidly in the early part of its life expectancy and then more slowly thereafter.

If you are a business entity, you may deduct non-collectable debts from your gross profit as an expense. If a boarder does not pay a boarding bill and you have to collect the money due by selling the horse at auction and the horse sells for less than what is owed, you can deduct the balance as a bad debt expense. A not-for-profit business will not be able to do that, as it is a level 3 expense.

If you are a business entity (sole proprietorship, partnership, S corporation or LLC), you may be able to reduce the tax liability of other income because you pass through losses from your business activity to your personal (1040) return.

You should research all the costs, expenses, market potential and customer base before starting a business of any kind, whether it be for profit or non-profit. You may decide that your part-time project should be a business for several reasons. The expense to operate the business and the income potential may make it necessary to be able to take advantage of depreciation, expensing and depletion.

You should consult with your accountant or CPA about how your business should be structured and whether it should be non-profit or profit. Careful planning at the beginning will reduce the stress of the 2 profit years in 7 year rule and the possibility of a hobby or business audit.

Horse owners that are in business are subject to capital gains tax if they sell a horse they have purchased during a twenty-four month period after they buy the animal unlike other assets that can escape capital gains after one year.

As an example; you purchase a futurity prospect in its yearling year for $10,000. Things go well as a two- year old and you win several prestigious events. Then someone offers you $70,000 for the horse at a show. Your mama didn't raise a fool and you nod your head up and down vigorously. That $60,000 is subject to capital gains tax instead of as ordinary income as it would be if you had held the horse for 24 months and one day.

If you are in the business of buying and selling horses, not keeping them longer than necessary, the above does not apply to you. In this case, horses are inventory and the income received is treated as ordinary income as with any business that buys and sells goods. However the expense you incur of getting the horse ready for resale is deductible. That includes feed, farrier, vet bills, and the cost of labor.

One of the questions I get from business owners is about how to arrive at a dollar amount to charge that will allow the horse business to survive over a period of time. There are three things that you must know in order to do this. Charging less than the competition is not one of them unless you truly have lower costs and overhead.

Overhead is a term we use to denote the amount of money needed each hour, day, week or month to keep the front doors open. It is the electricity, water, building rent or mortgage payment, taxes, insurance, etc. that we use whether we have customers or not. You need to know how much it costs each month for you to do this.

EXPENSES, DEPRECIATION, APPRECIATION

If you keep a set of books, (and you should) you should have this information available to you. If not, you should gather up all the checks and receipts for the past year and write down how much you spend each month on each item. Only then will you know how much it costs to keep the doors open.

You will find that it differs month to month and season to season. But if you have the amounts for each month, you can average them over a period of time. You will have a rough estimate of how much it costs each month to run your business.

Costs are expenses that vary month to month and season to season. A person running a boarding stable or training barn will have bedding, feed, farrier, vet, outside labor that are necessary to the business. Let us look at how we can control these expenses.

Bedding will vary from horse to horse. Some are pigs in the stall and some are not. Whatever you use for bedding, you want it to last as long as possible and be as dust free as possible. You should realize that some stalls are going to be picked two or three times a day in order to get the best use of the bedding.

Everyone says that they feed a coffee can of grain and one to three flakes of hay, two to three times a day. Go down to your bakers supply house and get a scoop with a scale built in to it. Buy a hanging scale and put it where you can weigh each flake of hay. Buy a weight tape and tape each horse when it comes into the barn. Start thinking about pounds of feed per animal. That estimated weight will help immensely in determining how much each horse should be fed during a 24 hour period. It takes 1.5 to 2 pounds of feed per 100 pounds of animal weight to maintain that horse depending on what it is doing.

Horseshoeing and veterinary charges are the responsibility of the horse owner. If you have to hold the horse for the shoer or vet, the owner should be charged a reasonable fee. Otherwise, they should be there for the shoeing and veterinary calls.

Costs are controllable. You need to shop around for the best price on feed each year. Prices will vary from supplier to supplier. Estimate how much grain and hay you will use over the next twelve months and contact each supplier to find his price to supply you.

The same applies to bedding. No matter what you use, if a supplier knows that you will use X amount of bedding over the next year, he will give you a better price than if you buy it one load at a time.

Profit margin is what we add on to our overhead and expenses to pay our salary and have something left over to cover unexpected emergencies or to grow our business. This is a sticky situation for most people. They want to meet or beat the competition but that may not be the answer if they want to maintain their business for an extended length of time.

If you want to have a 50% profit, you will add 100% to your overhead and costs. You can add more or less but that is your decision. Get out your old math books and look up the formulas. A 33% profit would require you to add 50% to your expenses.

If your business is boarding, you can add some extras that the competition may not do for a nominal fee or at cost as an incentive to your potential clients to board with you. If you are a trainer, you may do the boarding or hauling at a lower fee and raise your training fee to cover the difference. One should be innovative about these things. Wal-Mart does not sell everything at a lower cost than the competition. Some of their items have a profit margin of 90 % of more. The same thing will work for you. You can have low-price leaders but the rest of your product should be priced so you can have the profit you need to maintain your business.

Remember this formula to arrive at an approximate price to charge. Costs + overhead + percent needed to pay yourself and create a rainy day fund =selling price.

Depreciation Schedules
3 Year property depreciation
Horses used only for breeding, working or race purposes that are over 12 years of age when put in service as a business asset. Race horses regardless of age when put in service. It does not stipulate what breed. If you race Quarter Horses, Paints, Appaloosas, etc., you can depreciate them in three years.

5 Year property depreciation
Computers, computer printers, copy machines.
Trucks, horse trailers, business vehicle
Cattle, sheep, goats

7 year property depreciation
All horses that are 12 years or younger when you put them in service as a business asset
Office furniture and equipment, saddles, farm tractors, manure spreader, horse walker, granary, and fencing.

10 year property depreciation
Single purpose barn i.e. show barn, stallion barn, round pen barn, arena, hay storage, shavings storage. Any single purpose agriculture structure.

15 year property depreciation
Landscaping, trees and shrubs, roads, race track and special stock ponds

20 year property depreciation
Multi-purpose barns (stall and arena combined), non-agriculture buildings, tenant farmhouse.

30 year property depreciation
Real property

Depreciation is simply a way of recovering your investment over the expected useful period of an asset. It is a debit to your assets showing the perceived actual value of them. It is a credit to expenses allowing you to lower them

The more assets you can depreciate in the shortest amount of time is a goal that you should peruse. It will increase your net worth. As assets are depreciated, they are removed from your accrued deprecation and the asset is valued at its original cost, not at its depreciated value.

One of the more important deductions to happen recently is to allow racehorses to be three year depreciation regardless of age. You can recover your race horse investment and still deduct its expenses so if they don't win, you can dispose of them cheaply. Since we start training racehorses when they are about eighteen months old so that they will be ready to race as two year olds, this is an important change. It may sometime in future be used for futurity colts in other venues.

Let me give you an example of how depreciation works. It may or may not work in your particular case and you need to consult with a qualified accountant to verify if it does.

Having done some research and finding that a certain bloodline or discipline is doing very well on the national scene and there being an absence of that particular bloodline or discipline in my area, I decide to introduce it to my region. I attend sales that feature stock of the those bloodlines and end up purchasing a proven stallion and several producing mares as well as one or two younger horses that I believe to have the potential of being superior horses.

The stallion is 10 years old, has produced some foals that have gone on to a certain amount of fame and returned some money to their owners. His purchase price is $30,000. Of the mares that I have purchased and all of which are bred; one is 14 years old and the dam of offspring that have accumulated many points in their field; one is eight years old and her offspring are just starting out and is a five year old bred to a World Champion. Of the two young horses, one is a yearling and one is a two year old. The yearling is a gelding and the two year old is a started mare by the stallion I purchased.

Since I have mortgaged everything I own in order to assemble this group, I want to make a profit as soon as possible and keep the IRS at bay. This is how I am going to accomplish this.

My expenses for the year is $1800 per horses and that includes feed, farrier, vet, advertising and share of the mortgage, lights, water, electricity, etc. The stallion is used on my mares and he breeds 10 outside mares for $500 apiece plus mare care. The mares produce three foals that sell for a little money but not as well as I expected. The W/C sired colt goes for $2500 but the others only gross $2500 for the two.

My income looks like this for the year. Breeding fees bring in $5000 plus $1000 in mare care. Sales bring in $5000. My gross income for the year is $11,000. My outlay in expenses is $12,600 for the year. So, I am in the hole and the IRS is going to lay this one aside and want more documentation on whether I am a business or a hobby.

Using the MACRS (Modified Accelerated Cost Recovery System) depreciation schedule, I can lower my expenses and increase the bottom line on the P & L statement. It may still show a loss but it will be less. The stallion can be depreciated over seven years. Utilizing the MACRS depreciation tables, his first year depreciation is 14.29% of his purchase price or $4,287. The fourteen year old mare can be depreciated of over three years. Her purchase price was $10,000 and her first year depreciation is 33.33% or $3.333. The others can be depreciated over s seven year period including the two year old. The yearling gelding is the exception. He can only be expensed because he is not capable of reproducing.

It does not matter that someone else may have depreciated the horses before you bought it. When you buy that animal, you can start to depreciate the horse at the cost you bought it for. This applies to all depreciable assets.

On your balance sheet, you will increase your livestock asset and your accumulated depreciation (which is a debit from your gross assets). This will show the depreciated value of the livestock asset. On your Profit & Loss statement, you will show your income for the period and your expenses. Depreciation will be shown as a credit to your expenses which will lower your expenses.

In this particular example, my liabilities will increase by the amount of the loan and my net worth will be reduced.

I am often asked if you can depreciate an asset that you have purchased with a loan such as a truck or trailer. The answer is yes. Your liabilities will be increased by the amount of the loan and your asset accounts will be increased by the amount you purchased that asset for. The depreciation can be straight line or MACRS.

4

1031 Exchange of Horses

I discovered this way of acquiring better horses for my breeding program when I was studying for my real estate license. I didn't know if it would work for livestock but I did my research questioning my instructor and my attorney and found out that it would. Most people are like me and never really understand what can or can not be done. It pays off to expand your learning even when you think it will not apply to your business.

Everyone who has horses will want to acquire a better stallion or mares to add to the breeding program at sometime. The problem has been what to do with the present stallion. Do we sell him and maybe take a loss? Do we just put him out to pasture? Or do we geld him and hope that he will not continue to have his stallion manners? If you have someone interested in your stallion and you have another stallion identified that you want, this method may work for you. For years, people have invested in real estate and acquired bigger and better holdings while avoiding capital gains taxes by means of a 1031 exchange. You can apply the same practice to your horse business. The rules are simple and it does not take an expert to use them.

1. Like for like. It has to be a horse of the same sex and of equal or greater value. A stallion for one or more stallions, a mare for one or more mares, etc. Think about it. If your stallion is related to every mare you have, exchange him for a new one without having to lay out a bunch of money. Or upgrade your mare band by exchanging some of your mares for some of different bloodlines. Note: You Cannot Exchange Geldings or Spayed Mares.
2. After you have sold your horse to the buyer. You have 45 days to identify a replacement horse(s) and 180 days to complete the purchase.

There are three ways that this can be accomplished.

1. A direct simultaneous exchange between two parties.
2. Escrowed exchange. The seller asks the buyer to try to buy a third horse that is swapped for the first horse. A three-way swap that is somewhat cumbersome and may not be do-able.
3. Exchange using a qualified intermediary. Seller sells his horse. Seller places the funds with the intermediary. Following the above rules, seller finds the horse he wants and tells the intermediary. The intermediary tries to buy the horse for the price seller has told him that he wants to pay.

It is always a good idea to identify more than one horse in case the first deal can not be consummated. You can go on to number two and still get the deal done under the time limits.

If you as seller receives 'boot' in addition to a horse(s) that amount is subject to taxation. From my standpoint, you are better off to pay than to receive. You can depreciate the horse(s) on your regular depreciation schedule, 3 or 7 years.

Use of an intermediary removes the seller from any involvement with the buyer of the relinquished horse or the seller of the replacement horse. Intermediaries typically place the funds received from the horse being exchanged in a trust account until a replacement horse is purchased. They may or may not charge an additional fee for the transaction depending on whether they receive the interest from the account and what that interest may be. They will have a contract that you will sign before you give them the funds or indicate that you will give them the funds. Those contracts are negotiable to some extent but if the intermediary has been in business for some time, negotiable terms are few.

Where do you find a good intermediary? Ask your local real estate broker, banker or attorney. They can give you all the information you need on who may be willing to handle your transaction.

The IRS does not allow the following;

1. Exchange of horses of different sexes.
2. Your regular attorney, accountant or agent cannot act as your qualified intermediary. They can recommend someone but they cannot do it.

This is one of the ways you can improve your investment returns and increase the value of your overall holdings. There are many other ways of doing this. You could find a stallion that has the bloodlines and potential to be a great sire and form a syndicate with it as the principal horse. The members of the syndicate would buy breeding shares in the stallion and help pay for the cost of upkeep, showing and marketing the stallion, and in return get to breed mares to him based on the number of breeding shares that they have. If the stallion becomes popular, the price of foals would increase and thereby make the investment worthwhile.

Another way is to partner with someone who has capital to invest and buy a horse or horses to breed, show, race, etc. There are many people who want to be involved in horses but do not want to have the hands-on responsibility for caring for them. If you have a business plan that is doable, you can find investors from your sphere of acquaintances.

I had a client who bought from another client of mine a foal that was by one of my stallions. Over time I was able to bring them and the horse into my stable for boarding and training. When one of the mares I had bred was put up for sale, I mentioned it to her telling her how the mare was bred and the other facts about the mare. She bought the mare and I had another mare to breed and the produce was of exceptional quality and bought good prices in the market. We eventually formed a partnership with the client owning the mares and I owned the stallion. Such opportunities exist throughout the horse industry, one has to look for them and be ready to act when they appear.

If you are like me, you sometimes assume that what applies to other businesses does not apply to your horse business. But it does. Your horse business can use any and all of the benefits that other businesses enjoy if you treat it as a business. In recent years, there have been economic opportunities available to increase your profitability such as accelerated depreciation, a rise in the Section 179 deduction and many other ways to make your business profitable. You need to take advantage of these programs as they become available. To do this, you need to contact your accountant or CPA on a regular basis.

5

Bookkeeping and Records

In order to keep track of our income and expenditures, we need to have some sort of record. There are many software programs available to do this. Some of them are quite specialized. They track expenditures, depreciation, income, when you need to have your horses shod or wormed, show expenses, etc. Do you need all this? It depends on how many horses you have and what you do.

Your accountant will probably use one of the more traditional bookkeeping systems such as Quick Books. You can use them too and still track your expenditures and income. You must set up your accounts just as in any business but the headings will be different. If you do not know the difference between a credit and a debit, have your accountant help you.

You will want your accounts to track boarding income, training, hauling, service income such as consulting fees, commissions on selling a horse. You decide what you want but be sure to track all income at all times. In case of an audit by IRS, you can show what your income is.

Expense tracking are a necessary part of your accounting.

You should set up your books to track all the normal costs of running a horse business. Items such as feed, bedding, electricity, water, employees wages, FICA, federal withholding taxes, state taxes, vet fees, horseshoeing fees, show expenses, fuel for the truck and farm equipment are among the most common. You can set your books to track any expense you want and that will show on your tax forms. I have set my books up to track the number of horses I have each month. Why? So I can compare costs to the previous months or years and determine whether I need to raise my rates in order to maintain my profit margin.

You can show depreciation on a monthly or yearly schedule. There are certain rules that apply to depreciation set by the IRS. Every good bookkeeper knows them and can advise you on them, so I will not go into them here. If you choose to show depreciation on a monthly schedule, your bottom line may be in the black more often. If you are trying to impress the lending institution, you may want to do that.

I consider a most important item to have done monthly is a trial balance sheet (profit and loss statement). By doing this, you can see whether you are maintaining a profitable business or need to make changes in the near future. Just because you have a great cash flow does not mean that you are ending up with money in your pocket. You may be paying all the bills but are you generating a net profit? Often times, there is nothing left over to use in the future development of your business. Most accounting systems allow you to run a trial balance without having to close the books. By doing so, you or your bookkeeper can catch any mistakes that may have been made during the month. It is much easier to do this monthly rather than at the end of the year and trying to remember what went on.

Keeping track of your expense and income need not be an

onerous task. I keep a simple record of each horse and owner in a drawer in the tack room. The form can be created on the computer and should include owner's name and horse's name. Make a list of all the items that you do for owners and put them down the left side of the form. Items would be board, training, lessons, worming, vaccinations, horseshoeing, show fees, veterinary fees, blanketing, turn-out, holding the horse for the farrier or veterinarian, etc. Next you should have a space for the date you performed the services and what you charged the owner. At the bottom, you may want to make notations about the items listed such as split veterinarian calls or mileage you hauled the horse to a show. Anything that you think it is important to communicate to the owner. At the end of the month, I gather up all the sheets and take them to the bookkeeper who transcribes the items to the permanent record for the owner and invoices the owner. When the horse leaves the barn, I give a copy of the record to the owner so they know when to worm, have the feet done or give them their shots.

You should create a price list and post it where it can be easily accessible to the owners in your facility. You should, also, give one to the bookkeeper so that they can review the charges when they are posting items to the invoice. It will save you time and trouble when people question a charge on their bill. Often times, simple little things like this can save you from a lot of stress.

Good record keeping will pay off for you even if you hate it, like I do. If you have other employment or businesses, the necessity of records is most important. If you have an audit by the IRS (the likelihood of such a thing happening is always there), good records and books will help you prove that you are in the horse industry to make a profit. Lack of records and books may hurt your case and cause you to lose and have to pay large sums in back taxes. It is the little things like failing to keep a separate set of books for your business that will cause you problems. In fact it is one of the more common reasons for an adverse ruling by the Tax Court.

6

Business Review

At year's end, we sometimes breathe a sigh of relief that we have made it through another year without going broke or DID WE? Have we been too busy doing horse activities to really be mindful of how our business is doing? We have been able to pay the bills and one would think that your business is successful but we really don't know. I learned over the years that just because I had a lot of income and was able to pay the bills that it didn't mean that my business did not have problem areas that I should address.

Once a year we need to sit down with our business plan, support group (accountant, banker, attorney, insurance agent, etc.), our profit and loss statements for the last twelve months, and our balance sheets for the year and take a hard look at our business. It is time to plan how to improve our business, to rectify our misjudgments before they become too costly, to look at our bottom line and decide how to raise it.

First, compare this year's profit to last years. It should be improving if you are growing your business. Did you have to put in large sums of capital from your day job to support your horse business? Or were you able to take a salary from your horse enterprise? Were there items whose cost rose dramatically? Why? Beyond inflation, were there environmental conditions that caused your feed bill to rise or did it go down?

As horsemen, we do many different things to generate income. Did your income from your principal endeavor (boarding, training, lessons, breeding) increase or decrease? Which categories are increasing? Look for unprofitable products and services that are in need of revision in order to remain profitable or should be discontinued altogether.

If costs are starting to soar, are there ways that you can reduce them? Look for a different supplier of feed, supplements, bedding. Feed prices change dramatically from year to year or season to season. Hay is cheaper in summer and after the first of year because the grower wants to move his product and pay off his crop loans.

Is your overhead (electricity, water, etc.) increasing because you are leaving the lights on, have leaking waterers or the stall cleaners are using too much bedding? You must be aware of what is going on around the barn and in the marketplace. Find out what the competitors are paying for their supplies and what the suppliers are charging you. You should always be looking for a bigger discount if your demand for a product is increasing.

Remember you are in business and as an owner and employer; you want your business to be successful. Review your business plan, check to see if you are achieving your goals or not. Are your goals attainable? Or do you need to make changes in your programs? Do you need to add a different discipline to your lessons and training? Is your breeding program still successful? Are you selling your product in a timely manner?

Is it the time to change your inventory mix or add to what you have to offer to your customers? Be aggressive and innovative about what you have to offer the horse owning public. Do your market research and follow your instincts based on that research. Sometimes, we are afraid of changing for no other reason than we are comfortable with what we have. Do not be hesitant to try something new if you perceive that there is a demand that is not being met or that the public wants but it is not available in your area. Above all, do not let your personal desires and wants get in the way of adding something new. All of us have a certain breed or discipline that we are partial to but we should not let that be of major importance in deciding what to add or subtract from our product mix. What the customer wants and needs should be the deciding factor in what we offer at our facility.

Accountants are important at this time in helping us implement new changes in tax laws that have occurred in the last twelve months. They have studied the new changes and know which ones can help you and which ones can hurt you financially. They should have a good understanding of your business and its potential and its problems. Be open with them and discuss your business with your accountant. You never know when you may get an audit and both of you need to be knowledgeable of your business.

Attorneys should be aware of your potential liability or lack thereof. Discuss any new changes in your business and get their input from the start. Then if something does happen, you both will know what the outcome may be and can deal with it appropriately.

Appreciation can be used to help your case if you are audited. If the assets of the business increase in value even if the profit is minimal or non-existent, you can argue that you are a business. Consult your tax attorney on this.

Horses increase in value during the early years because of

training, showing or the bloodline suddenly becomes a hot item. Land generally increases in value while the improvements (buildings, etc.) depreciate over time. Improvements can increase in value if they are updated on a regular basis. You can increase the value by adding landscaping, ponds and roads, updating the facility, fences, etc. Remember that it is a deductible expense and can be depreciated over time.

You should consult with your insurance agent about the changes in your business. You may need to add more insurance to cover the items you are adding or less if you are removing some of the more dangerous conditions. The liability that horse businesses incur in the day to day operation of that business make it imperative that you keep up to-date with your insurance needs.

7

Contracts

The importance of a contract was driven home for me early in my career. I had leased a forty acre farm and converted the barn into stalls for my training and sale horses. I had thirty plus acres with nothing in them. A neighbor who had more horses than pasture came to me and wanted to rent the pasture area. I agreed and he moved his horses in. But he forgot to pay me. After several months of me hounding him for some sort of payment, he came and got his horses and still didn't pay me. That is when I found out that we didn't have a contract and I was left holding the bag, as they say. The importance of a piece of paper stating the terms of what each person would do in return for services was driven home. Many people think that a handshake constitutes a contract but in this time it is better to have it written down and signed by both parties to the transaction.

Another example of what can happen was brought to my attention recently. A young couple bought a boarding stable, where they had boarded their horses, after one of the elderly owners passed. The remaining owner was not into horses and put the place up for sale. The price was reasonable and they bought it. But there was a request, from the seller, that the help be allowed to stay as he had been there for a long period of time.

The couple, not wishing to move upon the property, agreed to this but neglected to get a contract with the help about his duties and what was expected in return for housing for him and his horses.

In due time, the help was injured by one of the new owners horses (supposedly) and he promptly sued them and their insurance. He continued to live on the property in spite requests by the new owners to leave. The outcome was he had to be forcibly evicted and a lawsuit had to be settled.

All of this could have prevented by having a contract with him and a rental agreement.

There are two types of contracts, verbal and written. Both are legal----but if you have a verbal contract with a person and something happens where you must go to court to enforce the contract, the burden of proof is with the petitioner. It is what each party said and did, backed up by documentation (something of value was exchanged, actions by both parties, etc.) that the presiding judge has to use to reach his decision.

Either party can write contracts. They can be as simple or as complex as you want them to be. They can be drawn up by an attorney (recommended) or written by the parties. There are books written that have sample contracts in them that can be used. Even if you do so, it is good ideas to have your attorney look them over before you sign them. Those contracts are universal and may not hold up in court in your state. They need to be tweaked a bit to conform to your state laws and to slant them in your favor by your attorney.

When I am entering into a business agreement with an owner, I sometimes jot down what I think they said. If I don't comprehend what they are saying, I will ask them if they are saying such and such. What I am doing is repeating back to them what I understood them to say. They can confirm or deny that is what they are saying.

Once I have down what they are asking me to do in exchange for money or whatever, I look it over and put it in a contract form. I then present it to them and ask them to look it over and make any changes that they want. When they give it back to me, I call my attorney or drop it at his office and have him go over it before I sign it.

I have a reason for contacting my attorney. I don't want to lose the farm because I signed a contract that I shouldn't have. Accidents happen and things change. I don't want to be responsible for something that I couldn't prevent or that I misunderstood. My property is as safe as I can make it but horses and clients still manage to get hurt. It happens with my horses and it happens with your horses. What may be relevant at the time of the contract may change or people may fall upon hard times and renege on a deal. If you do not have a contract, how are you going to get your money? A written contract gives you a place to start.

People tell me from time to time that they don't use contracts and they have never been sued. They are among the fortunate few but when I delve into their operation, it is because of the lack of knowledge by the other party that has kept them from being sued more than luck. They post limited liability signs but since neither party knows what the law actually says, they get away with it.

The universal contracts have a clause alluding to the laws of your state. They do not have a security clause because the law differs from state to state. But, if you or the other party doesn't know the laws, how are you going to enforce the contract. See your attorney first and this won't happen.

In this time where litigation is rampant, it is common sense to get it in writing at the beginning of each transaction. Each party involved should consult with his attorney to insure that everything is covered and nothing is left out.

If you are running a boarding, training or breeding business, there are several things that should be included in the contract. You should have all of the pertinent information such as what you will do in exchange for money, what you will provide in terms of care and feed, who is responsible for damage to the premises by an animal, security deposit, hours of operation, what to do in case of an emergency, etc. A security clause establishing your interest in the horse is necessary so if you do have to use the judicial system to collect your money there will not be any doubt as to your claim.

There is a time period in which you have to peruse legal action. If you do not act within that period, you will not be able to collect the debt or remedy the situation. The contract should spell out what will happen and who will pay the costs of the actions taken to satisfy the debt.

If you have an attorney, he can advise you about the course of action for you to use. Do not overlook the small claims court. You can usually take small amounts, under $5000, to that court and achieve satisfaction of your claim. In most cases, you do not need your attorney present but he can advise you about what you will need to present to the judge.

If you are a horse owner who uses a boarding stable, trainer, contract hauler, etc., I would urge you to get it writing before you do anything. Find out what is covered by their insurance, what type of service they provide, additional costs that you may have to pay and so on.

If you are a business, put it in writing and explain to the

customer every item in the contract. Answer their questions truthfully. Do not be afraid of losing a potential client by hemming and hawing around. If they don't like your contract, thank them for considering you and be happy that you still have the farm. Lawsuits are costly and you may not always win.

Having said all this, if you still want to use a verbal contract for whatever reason, at least jot down the pertinent matters you discussed with the other party and have them sign and date it. Changes should be initialed and the document put in a safe place. Then, if and when you need to refresh your memories, you will have a document to refer to. And maybe you won't have to go to court over a simple transaction.

The importance of having something in writing can not be over emphasized. Time passes and I don't know of anyone who has a perfect memory. What you say and what the other party says can be misconstrued by either one of you.

The stress, time wasted and money spent on a case can be alleviated by taking a few moments to get it in writing. You can have your attorney draw up a contract and use it with a majority of customers. It will contain what the terms are, what happens if one of the parties defaults, a clause that states the provider has a security interest in case of default and any other items that you, as a provider of services or goods, feels necessary.

By using an attorney, the contract will be worded to comply with your state's laws. This is most important. The forms that are in some books and on the internet are so generalized that they are more or less useless if you are confronted with having to pursue the judicial system for a remedy to your problem.

One other point that must be discussed is the use of a UCC. It declares to anyone who may have an interest in purchasing an animal that you are boarding, training or selling on payments that you have a legal interest in the animal.

Uniform Commercial Code (UCC) administers several statutory liens, including state and federal tax liens, employment warrants and farm liens in crops or livestock because of labor performed, materials supplied, or services rendered.

The most prevalent filing by the public is the Agricultural Services Lien, which is a statutory lien claiming a security interest provided to aid the growing or harvesting of the crops or the raising of animals.

Most liens that apply to horses are possessory liens that secure payment for service on the horse. There are four types of lien that apply specifically to horses.

1. Agister's lien; anyone who has possession of/or takes care of horses for another person/entity, including boarding stables, trainers. You do not have to go to court, just post notice in a prominent place in barn and hope the client can pay the bill. If after a reasonable time, the bill is not paid you can initiate a proceeding to sell the horse at public auction to pay the bill. There are time limits when proceedings can occur therefore you should check with your attorney before initiating any action.
2. Horse breeder's lien.
3. Veterinarian's lien
4. Farrier's lien

The importance of a security agreement and a signed promissory note as part of the contract is important. Don't forget to register an UCC with the state. These items will save you time and attorney fees. Final note: you must act in a timely manner to enforce your lien rights. I recommend you consult your attorney immediately.

I have received several inquiries about selling on contract from horse owners who need to get rid of their surplus and still want to make a profit or at least break even. In this time of slow market conditions, supply greater than demand and many horse breeders who are dispersing their stock, one should be looking for different ways to market their product. Offering to sell on contract may work for you if you act in a business-like manner and do your research.

Selling on a contract can be profitable if you follow some simple rules. It is important to get everything in writing. You can use the sample contracts you find in books on horse businesses or procure one at your local office supply to act as a guide. You should check with your attorney about the laws in your state before you begin or have him do it for you. You would want to have the attorney review it before presenting it to the prospective buyer.

Get a credit check upfront. You should ask the prospective buyer to sign a credit application, (available at most office supply stores), so you can legally look into his references and check with his creditors. You can check their credit with one of the credit reporting bureaus using the information provided on the credit application. Credit reports are available online for a small fee.

The contract should have some very specific language in it. It should have the buyer's address, phone number, closest relative and their address and phone number, and where the horse will be stabled, (address, city, state). The seller's address, phone number should be in the contract.

A complete description of the horse(s) that is being sold, such as height, weight, color, age, registration number, health certificate, etc. Take photos of the animals on all four sides.

Give one set of photos to the buyer and keep one set for your records.

The contract and promissory note should state the down payment, length of time involved, the interest rate, which person pays if you have to repossess the horse, type of insurance required by seller and a security clause. You should It should be signed both by the buyer and seller and each should have a copy.

Every contract should have an interest rate. You are loaning money that you could use for other things. Charge the going interest rate for loans. The buyer may pay off the loan earlier to avoid paying the interest. In addition to signing the contract, you should have the buyer sign a promissory note so there is not any doubt that he owes you money. If you do not charge any interest or fail to get a promissory note from the buyer, a court or the IRS could rule against you in complaint or audit.

The down payment can be any amount that you want but is typically 20 to 25%. It should be a sufficient amount to insure that the buyer has a monetary interest in the horse. A low down may move your horse faster but may work against you. The buyer may not feel responsible to make any payments beyond the down. The buyer should be made to feel that it is in his best interests to make the payments. The contract should state what happens to the down payment if the buyer does not make the payments or defaults on the contract for any reason.

From my personal experience, a security clause or a separate page containing the security phrasing is most important. It states that you have a financial interest in the horse until he is paid for and you release your interest in the horse. Lack of such documentation means that if the buyer defaults, you have to go to court and prove that you have a financial interest in the animal. This expense is often the reason that sellers do not pursue legal action. You should not assume that you can just go and take the horse without legal documentation giving you permission to do so.

Insuring the animal is not different from insuring your vehicle. It is the buyer's responsibility and the seller is the named beneficiary until the horse is paid for. Mortality, accidental death or anything that renders the animal unusable for the original purpose intended is to be considered. Sellers should be adamant about this as they don't have control of the horse or its surroundings. If something happens to the horse, the buyer often feels that his contract to pay for the horse is over. In order to prevent this; insure the animal for the sale price. You can always reduce the amount owed the seller by the payments made and the buyer can keep the residual amount.

The contract should spell out in very specific wording what is expected as to maintenance of the horse during the course of the contract. Worming, shots, general care of the animal are items that are seldom addressed in contracts and are often the cause of seller remorse. If it is important to you, either as the seller or buyer, have it put into the contract before you take sell or take possession of the animal.

I find that sellers, of horses on contract, seldom file an UCC (Uniform Commercial Code) with the state when they sell the horse. An UCC effectively gives notice to the public that you have a financial interest in the horse. The cost is small in relation to the selling price and should be done immediately upon closing the sale. If the horse is to be domiciled in another state, you should file a UCC in that state as well as the state where the sale took place.

Leases with option to buy contracts are similar to a sale contract. The same criteria should be used with the addition of the lease period and amount to be paid for the lease. The period of the lease should be reasonable. Forty five to 60 days should be sufficient for the prospective buyer to evaluate the horse and its suitability to the buyer's purpose. The lease payments can be applied to the down payment in full or part if the option is picked up. If the option is not picked up, then all lease monies should become the property of the seller.

8

Insurance

One of the biggest expenditures a horse business has is insurance. Many owners try to get by with as little as possible believing that the limited liability statue protects them. First, you should know that all equine limited liability laws have one thing in common. If you furnish the tack, equipment, or horse, and the participant is injured, you are at risk even if you have the person sign a release of liability. If you fail to make reasonable and prudent efforts to determine the ability of the participant, you can be held liable. If your facility has a dangerous latent condition which is known or should have been known and you failed to post warning signs, you are liable. If you or your employees commit an act or omission and that act or omission causes injury to the participant, you can be held liable for that. An insurance agent who understands the needs of a horse business and is interested in providing you with the coverage you need is of utmost importance.

As small business owners, one of the problems we have is deciding whether we need or can afford insurance. The premiums seem to be more than we will able to recover since we are not going to ever use it. That is why we have limited liability signs on the barn and arena.

I know that everyone who comes in my barn to look at a horse will tell me all about their ability to ride. Yeah, right! Would they stretch the truth, just a little? Would my grooms tell them how gentle the horse is? Of course! They want to get paid at the end of the month just like everyone else.

What if the stall cleaner leaves the stall door open and the stallion decides to go look the ladies over? Or, I forget to not feed the N/H mare alfalfa? Or, a client's horse has colic or worse while he is in the trailer headed for a show?

There are a multitude of potential events that can and do happen every day to horses and their owners. When you are with friends and colleagues, what you talk about is the bad things, not the good things that have happened to horses in your charge or someone else.

In order to prevent someone from owning our assets, which we have labored to build and hopefully to use as our retirement, we should have coverage that will prevent that from happening. There are a number of things that happen for the simple reason that we are dealing with an animal. It does not have the reasoning powers of a human but responds to their basic instincts which are very different than humans.

We should have commercial equine liability insurance that covers our employees and ourselves against accidents caused by errors and omissions. It should also cover the buildings and contents against natural disasters, fire, earthquakes, floods, etc.

The average homeowner's policy will not cover commercial equine activities whether you are in business or not. Sometimes a not-for-profit business can get a 'rider' to cover their horse activity but not always. You should check with your agent first before assuming that your horse activities are covered.

People who board, train and care for horses, as a business,

should have care, custody and control insurance for non-owned horses in their care. Even if the owner signs a waiver, you are legally responsible for the well-being of the horse while it is in your custody. This insurance will cover accidents that can occur in the barn, at a show or race and in transporting horses.

The above two policies are the most important in my experience to have if you are in the business of training and boarding. If you are a breeder, you may want to have additional coverage to protect your investment.

Most breeders should have full mortality insurance on the principal stallion and mares, (producers who provide you with the bulk of your income). The coverage will pay in case of accident, injury or death of the animal with some exclusions. Usually it is available for a nominal fee and the animal can be quite young. It is something to consider if you are buying potential stallions or broodmares. If an injury or death occurs, you can recover some of the investment you have made in the animal. You may also want fertility insurance on the stallion and/or mares. If for some reason the stallion or mare is unable to reproduce, you can recover some of the investment lost by that occurrence.

You can insure your business for almost anything you want but you should use good judgment if you are in business. One should talk to a knowledgeable bloodstock agent about what is available. Ask the agent about what types of coverage other individuals that he services have.

Short war story. At one of the seminars, a participant told me that they were willing to forego insurance because they were on a fixed income (retirement) which was not at risk. They had a stallion, boarded horses and gave lessons to supplement this income. What they were risking was the farm and the rest of their assets. Many of us would not be willing to put our most important asset (farm) at risk. We want the asset to provide us with some income.

There are instances that the client (owner of the horse) should be advised that they should insure the horse themselves. There are circumstances such as colic, inherited genetic diseases, unforeseen accidents that will result in an emotional and monetary loss to them.

Novice horse owners often assume that if anything happens to their horse in your care, your insurance will reimburse them. You should inform them at the beginning of your relationship what might happen to their horse and what your insurance may cover. Then allow them to decide whether they should have insurance themselves on the animal.

Spread the insurance burden with others. If you have independent trainers or instructors in your barn, ask them to provide insurance on themselves for their activities. You should not have to cover independent actions of others. Be sure that you have a copy of their coverage and that your insurance agent also has a copy in his files.

Insurance should be considered as an investment rather than a burden. You are protecting your assets against disasters that can bankrupt you. It is an expense that is deductible and desirable if you are building an estate to help you send your children to college, build a retirement resource and have an enjoyable lifestyle.

You should sit down with your insurance agent and review the past year with them. Horse businesses are changing all the time. You may not have the stallion but you have only mares and geldings. You may not train rail horses but are now doing working horses. You may have erected separate hay and bedding storage building. All these things can decrease or increase your liability and your agent should be aware of them so they can be sure that you have the right coverage.

9

Independent Contractors or Employees

Outside labor, whether independent contractor or employees, has to be used unless you have a large extended family involved in your horse enterprise. Why? No person wants to or can work 24/7 without a break now and then. You will want to attend a horse function or just take a vacation away from the business and in order to do this; you must have someone to do the chores.

The problem is to find someone, who has an interest in horses, is dependable, responsible and will work on an as-needed basis. You can sometimes find a client who wants to do these things part-time in an exchange for a reduction of their bill. The down side is they may not have the experience and when you have to stop their participation; you lose both your help and a client. Only you can make that decision. I have found that it is easier to hire an independent contractor or employee whose livelihood is taking care of animals for owners. If they don't work out, I can terminate the contract and find someone else.

Independent contractors are contracted at an agreed upon price to do certain jobs such as clean stalls, exercise horses, repair stalls or fence, etc. You do not have to furnish the tools for them or set the hours they work to do the contracted job. You do not have to have workman's compensation for them but you should have liability insurance and tell them of any dangers they may face in dealing with the horses in your barn such as a horse that kicks or is defensive of its space. If you do any thing such as set the hours when they work or provide equipment or any benefits, they may be viewed by the IRS as employees.

You have no control over an independent contractor (stall cleaner, riding instructor, trainer) but you should have a contract stating the work to be done, the hours during which work shall be done, the amount of compensation for such work and how the agreement can be terminated. Do not offer any benefits to independent contractors, to do so will red flag the IRS that they are employees.

If control over the people who work for you is important to you then employees may be the answer. You will have to pay a going wage. If you live in a minimum wage state, you will have to pay that. You will pay the employers share of the federal and state taxes. You will be expected to pay for overtime and holidays. You will have to furnish workman's compensation in most states in case one of your employees is injured on the job. You will need to keep a record of hours worked, whether the employee is full-time or part-time, payroll deductions, etc.

If you are going to have employees, you should have your attorney draw up an employment contract stating the nature of the work, duties of the employee, hours of work, compensation. That is the minimum, he may suggest more.

You should have a company handbook written to give your

employees. It should have the company policy, employee's duties, who to contact in case of injury, a clause on sexual harassment in the work place, who to contact with a complaint, conditions that will cause you to terminate the employment etc. Now you know why you need an attorney to help you.

Often you will wonder when you are going to get to train horses, give lessons, or any of the things that you like to do because of the paperwork involved with employees. The best way to handle this is to delegate someone to handle the paperwork and you attend to the functions of running your business. The person can be a member of the family who has computer experience and bookkeeping software such as QuickBooks. Or you can hire a person whose sole job is to do records. Depending on the size of the facility and number of clients, the job may be part-time and if the person has an interest in horses, there are other duties that they can do.

Anyone who is not an employee (such as your farrier or veterinarian) whom you pay more than $600 in a year should be issued a 1099 showing how much was paid and reported to the IRS. Again this will show that you are in business and not a hobby. And don't be surprised if the independent contractor quits the minute you tell them this. Anyone who has a large cash flow may not want the IRS know how much they actually make to avoid taxes. If the contractor is a legitimate business, they won't have a problem with this but if it is their part time job that may be another story.

10

Marketing

Every business owner wants to attract customers to his store. It is not any different if you have a horse related business. Whether you own a farm, boarding stable, train horses for the public, have a feed and tack store or any of the other businesses that depends on the horse owning public.

Some think that if you have an Internet website, that is all you have to do. They have the assumption that the public will find you eventually and your business will prosper. Most find out that it takes more time than you have available to make your business profitable.

Your advertising should include all available forms of the media. Print, TV spots, sponsorships of classes at horse shows, press releases, websites, etc.

Print media are magazines, newspapers, directories, posters, and flyers among other forms of printed matter. Your advertising budget should include this form of advertising as a priority. You can use print to advertise your website, upcoming events that you will be participating in, what your horses and owners are doing, open houses and other happenings at your place of business. You can advertise your horse for sale, special offerings of items or services, tack, and a multitude of other things that are horse related.

Most magazines have special rates for 3-6-12 month advertising. It does not have to be the same size each month. In fact, some magazines will let you carry a business card ad as part of your contract and give you the reduced rate. Always ask the sales representative what is the best rate they have available and what it consists of. How many photos, type of print, special promotions, (stallion issue, foal issue, etc.), that may be of help to you in advertising your business.

If you use a logo or catch phrase to describe your operation, use it consistently in every piece of advertising you do. This includes printed matter and your Internet site, TV ads, sponsorships, etc. Plan your advertising in advance. You should determine what your budget is for the year, what media you will use, and the size of each ad.

Showing or exhibiting your horses can be a form of advertising. Stallion auctions can be used as an advertising tool. Futurities can be useful in exhibiting your foals especially if you own the stallion and the foals are excellent representatives of your breeding program. If you are a trainer, showing the results of your training programs can be helpful in securing new customers and securing sponsorships from feed, tack and trailer manufacturers.

TV spots are available on your local cable provider at a very reasonable cost. They show programs that are suitable to their area's viewing audience. In order to recover some of the cost of doing so they sell spots to local advertisers. These spots are dispersed throughout the program in place of the national advertising. You can pick the programs that you want your ads to appear in and reach a larger audience that is interested in horses and the industry as a whole. The cable provider probably has their own production company to film your ad but if they don't, ask your local TV station if they have someone who does it for them. The money you pay for this service may seem high but you own the ad and it is professionally done. Home video does not work unless you are a very talented amateur. Hire a good announcer to do your voice over on your ad. Nothing turns people away like a poorly produced video.

A very useful piece of advertising is not really advertising. It is the use of press releases to your local newspaper and TV station about things happening at your business. I learned when I first got started and money was tight, that I could call the local newspaper and ask them if they would be interested in a story about what was going on in my barn. I only did this when something was going on that was news worthy. There is a difference between being news and just bragging. A World champion is news, selling a horse for a zillion dollars is news, having a new foal is news if it is a slow week or day. Talking about how many horses you have or how you beat the competition at a schooling show is just bragging. If you know the difference and only call the news editor or director when it is pertinent or people oriented, in time they will call you to see if you have something going on that is news.

Internet web sites are just another tool of advertising. They should not be the only tool. Most of us are capable of building a web site using one of the many software products available and our ISP's web server. Take time to analyze what your site is to look like and what content you want it to have. In a time, where imitation is rampant, make yours look original. If you use the free sites, you may as well use your time doing something more useful. There are millions of them that do not receive many hits if any.

If you do not feel that you can produce a suitable site, contract with a reputable person who has sites that are running. Look at the sites, ask the owners if they are satisfied with their site and ask for references. There are many people advertising themselves as web designers who have only produced one site, their own. Find out what search engines they use and how to get your site on as many search engines as possible at a reasonable cost.

Use of print media such as magazines who have an Internet site can work in your favor. For a small fee, they will post your ad on their site and post a link to your web site. So you not only get print coverage and internet coverage, you get potential customers to your homepage.

Open houses or clinics held by you at your farm, barn or stable is another form of publicity that entices the potential client to your business. To have a successful open house or clinic, one must utilize all of your advertising resources. Advertise your event well in advance of the date it is to be held. Ads should appear in print, press releases to the local newspapers, TV and your web site. If you have door prizes or special offers put them in your ads. What you want to happen is to entice people who have never seen your business to come and shop. You should have someone, who is familiar with your operation; greet them when they come in. If they have questions, answer them honestly and as quickly as possible. Your barn should be clean and in good shape. Broken fences, dirty stalls and poorly lit arenas will diminish the impression that you are trying to present.

Above all, be consistent with your advertising. Marketing is one of the areas that you should pay attention to in order to create a presence in the area. Your name in front of the consumer at all times in some manner will enhance your ability to be profitable and have a steady flow of customers. You want people to think of you when they want to buy, breed, have a horse trained, board a horse or take a lesson.

Reviewing your marketing plan at the end of the year is appropriate. If you have tracked your advertising through the year, you know which media and ads were the most cost effective for the year. You should make up your advertising calendar for the coming year using the data you have gathered. Ask the sales personnel of the various media what they are featuring each month, what discounts are available, what are their deadlines, etc.

Do not put your entire advertising dollar in just one media. Exposure to the public is paramount in keeping your business alive and well. Inexpensive business card or directory ads will help your business to stay in front of the public everyday all year long. Don't overlook the opportunity to bring your business to the public through news stories in your local or regional papers about what you have won or what your clients have done. Let us review some things. You should always have a marketing plan for your product or service. It should be written down so you can show it to your bank, attorney and accountant. It will help everyone be on the same page.

When you write your plan, it should include some items that will help you throughout the year.

1. Do a SWOT analysis. You will list your strengths, weakness, opportunities and threats of your business. Doing this will help you realize what areas you need to improve on and what areas you are very strong in.
2. Know what your competitive advantage is. What do you do or sell that is unique to your business.
3. Research your marketing options. Learn what type of

advertising works in your area. Print? Internet? TV? Combination? It will help you spend your advertising dollar more effectively.

4. Know your market intimately. You should be aware of who uses your service or product and why. You should have input from those customers about what they desire that is different from what you now have. You should be prepared to meet that need.

5. Be consistent with your marketing message, image and logo. Much too often, business people do not give their advertising enough time to work. They will try something and if it does not generate an instant response, they will give it up and try something else. You have to give advertising time to reach your potential customer and for them to respond to it. The same type of ad running on a consistent basis, whether monthly, bimonthly or seasonal, will develop recognition and with that, you will get customers.

6. Track your marketing effectiveness throughout the year. By doing this, you will get a sense of what is working for you and whether you need to change your marketing. You can see if your advertising dollar is being spent wisely.

7. Put together an annual calendar. By using the above items, you should be able to put together a calendar of when and what you want to advertise. Seasonal, slack time specials, whatever. It will give you an idea of how much you want to spend each month on advertising and where you want to place that advertising.

11

Improving Your Business

Everyone is talking about the horse market and what is going on. Breeders are downsizing or dispersing programs, people are not buying like they did in the 90's, etc. War stories abound. What everyone forgets or doesn't acknowledge is the horse business is a cyclical industry that is dependent on the economy.

I have been in this industry for over 50 years and I have not seen an opportunity like this in the last twenty-five years. I feel now is an opportune time for people who have wanted to get into the horse business or those who have not achieved the success that they wanted. There are some great buys around if you are looking to improve your breeding programs, get some quality prospects for your clients if you are a trainer, to expand your client base if you give lessons or to buy that dream horse farm. Interest rates have never been lower, depreciation has been accelerated. What more could you ask for?

But the real question is how do we market what we have in the barn and not take a loss while we improve our programs whether they are training, breeding, lessons, etc. We must point out to potential customers the advantages of purchasing now.

Also, we need to take every advantage of any tax incentives offered that will improve our business. In a changing world, we need to be innovative; to do things a little different than we used to.

Become the bank. You can sell your horses or services on payments if you take time to act like your bank or loan company. Get a credit report on the person before you commit to selling. You won't lose the sale if the person is honest and wants to buy your horse. If he doesn't want to fill out a credit application, you are probably money ahead. Get an iron-clad contract drawn up by your attorney with a security clause, interest rate, payments (when, where and how much), what happens if the buyer doesn't perform as agreed, what happens if the horse becomes ill, dies or becomes unusable. File an UCC (Uniform Commercial Code Agriculture Lien) immediately upon a contract sale in your own state and the state where the horse is going. This serves notice on any one who buys the horse later on that there is a lien against it. If the horse is paid for in full you can release the UCC. If not, at least you have the groundwork in place to go get your money or the horse.

Talk to your bank manager about processing credit cards. If they don't do it, ask them to recommend a third party credit card processor. For the 3% or whatever they charge, you can create a cash flow. In reality you are servicing the customer who may want to pay all his bills once a month. The worry is eliminated of whether the check is good or not for you. Those of you who are trainers or give lessons, this will help you gain customers who may be short of funds right now but have a high limit credit card. Sellers of horses will also benefit for the same reasons.

Advertise that you accept credit cards. You may be the only one in your area who does. That opens your business to new customers who want to buy but do not have the necessary funds right now. If you have a web site or sell horses on the Internet, you can get an account with Pay Pal that is relatively inexpensive. You will pay a small fee for this service but it is well worth it. A third party credit service can transfer the funds to your checking account in a relatively short time and thus you improve your cash flow.

Let everyone know who you are and where you are. Advertise in the regional and national print media. If you have a web site, put it in the print media so they can pursue your site and see what you have in more detail. But with the enormous list of sites available for horses, you must let the public know about yours, so put it every paper you advertise in and some of the local ad publications (newspaper, nickel ads, whatever).

Last, adjust your thinking to fit the times. You know that your product has worth but is it competitive? If you have been pricing your product on the basis everyone else is asking this much, it is time for you to take a hard look at your operation. There is a lot of overpriced product on the market today and the consumer is not going to pay a high price just because you think it is worth that. Be honest with yourself and your operation. If you need to change it, change it. At some recent sales, I have seen owners turn down a good offer for a difference of $150 -$200. The upkeep in the next month will eat up that difference. If the offer is reasonable, nod your head up and down vigorously.

One of hot items is terms of selling your horse is to consign it to one of online auctions or to have one featuring your program. As we move into the tech age in the horse business, it is nice to have one more way to sell our horse.

To begin with, I would suggest you consign to one of the online businesses that are doing it. If you are an established business, you may want to contract with one of the auctioneers that will sell for you online. They do the work and you get to play with your horses.

You should be prepared to have a video of your horse doing what he does best and a conformation picture or video for the auction house.

Know what is going on in your region economically and what is going on in other regions and nationally. Take time to talk to others in the business and learn from them. If your product needs changing, change it. Add services or bloodlines that are in demand by your clients. Look at your pricing and overhead, now is the time to adjust them and strive to lower your day to day expenses. Everyone is in the same situation. Be aggressive, ask for discounts, better prices on things, shop around and compare prices. The best deal may be in your back-yard and not on the Internet.

Most of all be optimistic. Remember it goes in cycles and it will come around. You just have to be ready for it.

12

The Horse Market

As I am writing this, the fervor over reopening the kill plants in different states, (in the US), has the populace in an uproar. Governors, movie celebrities, animal groups are beating the drums and stirring up the general public. And now the judicial system is ruling on actions that are further delaying solving a problem. One, in my opinion, that is going to get worse.

The general public perceives that a horse is a pet and should be treated like a 1000# dog or cat. That assumption is allowing the extremists to accomplish their goals. But, horse people everywhere are going to feel the results as our horses will be taxed, restricted to certain areas, and have to buried in private disposal areas.

To top it all off, the BLM has its own little breeding program going. They were appointed guardians of the wild horse, (notice; I did not say MUSTANG. There are not any!). They are producing more than they can sell and they are now warehousing them on large tracts of land for vast sums of money.

We are shipping over 175,000 horses a year to slaughter houses that are located in Canada and Mexico. The Indian reservations are being swamped with horses that are being abandoned by their owners. We must arrive at a solution to the problem soon. The competition for customers to buy horses has greatly increased. And the public is paying for this.

Another problem that is going to accelerate the overabundance of horses is the three year depreciation of racehorses. You can buy a prospective racehorse and if he does not work out (most of them don't), you can give him away at the end of the depreciation period..

For years the price of horses depended on the price of cattle. If cow prices were high, as they are now, so was the price of horses. But, they were cheaper than cattle and as such, they were attractive to the European market that does not have the same view as the US. In fact, during WWII, we ate horse meat and did not die from it.

I live in an area that has a large population of Amish and Mennonite horsemen. It has a large population that trail rides and does other recreational riding as well as several large ranches. In this area, there is still a reasonable demand for buggy horses (translation; Standardbreds that did not make it on the track), trail horses and working cow horses.

We are still extricating our nation from a recession that impacted our way of living. We have had to make major decisions regarding the way we live.

One of the items impacted has been the recreational use of the horse. Owners are trying to sell, give away or otherwise dispose of their horses. Breeders are downsizing or disposing of their horse programs because of the low selling price and the higher cost of feed and care. In former times, these animals would have gone to Europe and the market would have adjusted to fewer animals.

Now the rescue groups (non-profit businesses) are buying them and reselling them to the public by adopting them out.

The hobby horse breeders keep on producing animals of little or no value and flooding an overstocked market, driving prices even lower.

If the average horse owner would try to be more innovative and try different ways to market their product as well as reduce the number of horses they produce, they will survive the current downturn in the market. Let me suggest a few ways that may work for you.

The current currency exchange rate can work for you. The overseas market that hesitated to invest in US horses before, can and will buy horses now. Why? Their currency will buy a better horse than before. But that horse must have those qualities that set it apart from the rest. Here in the states, studs and mares that are by leading sires are still bringing very good prices. The ones that are not by studs that have not done or produced anything worth noting will bring prices that are considerably lower.

Instead of being a farm, consider becoming a business. You can do so much more if you are a S Corporation or LLC than if you are not plus you can shield your assets. You can depreciate the horses you buy, farm equipment, trucks, trailers, your computer and supplies, barn and arenas, plus much more. You can expense your feed, farrier, show expenses, office supplies and the list goes on and on. While your profit may be minimal, at least you can show a profit in most cases.

You may want to geld old super stud, making a useful gelding that has some value in the marketplace. You can always breed the mares to a stallion that has done something and thereby increase the value of the foals. If you have not noticed, geldings are bringing better prices than fire-breathing studs, halter broke broodmares and those horses under a year old. The well broke gelding will always be in demand. Horses that have some sort of training will bring a better price regardless of the market.

If you have excess stalls or pasture with available hay, consider letting the animal control people know that you can take care of X number of animals. As time goes on, there will be a greater demand for that type of facility. While you won't get rich, you generate income in addition to your present income. Once it becomes known that you take in horses, you will have more horses that you wished. If possible, charge the owner for taking in the horse. Pick the horses you take in. Do not take every horse just because it is free.

Those with serious health or mental issues are not worth dealing with. Suggest to the owner that they have the animal euthanized. They will moan and groan but it is still the logical thing to do. Sell them a plot to bury the horse and charge an annual fee for grounds upkeep. It may be a better alternative to the rendering plant for many horse lovers. You can become a retirement facility providing complete care for the aged horse providing for his last years and then bury him in your cemetery.

I am sure that there are many other ways to deal with horse population and as time goes on, people will think of them. The NAIS system will come to pass and give us a better estimation of the true horse populace in the US. It will severely limit the switching of registered animals and be able to track animals in and out of the country. It will also enable us to identify those animal that carry disease or genetic defects and limit the export and import of those animals. The states that tax the sales of horses will be able to do so more easily.

In order to increase the price of horses, horse breeders and horse owners should do three things. 1. Decrease the numbers of horses. 2. Produce horses that are salable. 3. Become more active (either pro or con) in promoting the the changes that will occur in the horse industry.

13

Board of Advisors

The most expensive sentence you will ever utter is, "I don't have the money right now," or "I didn't know that I could not or could do that." What you do not do or know because it takes a little money or time can cost you. You can lose your farm, your credit, have liens placed against your assets and lose your reputation.

Every business needs a support group or board of advisors to help it grow and prosper. Each member of this advisory committee should have expertise in his chosen field and be willing to share that expertise.

As you put together your advisory group, one of the concerns is how does one find someone with horse experience as well as being an accountant, attorney, insurance agent, etc. If you take the concern about horse experience away, what would you look for? Someone who comes well recommended with experience at a variety of situations in his field. That is what most of us in business should look for when considering someone for advisory group.

You need to search for an accountant that has extensive

experience with many types of businesses, not just a bookkeeper who will post income and expenses where you tell them to. An experienced accountant will know what you can deduct, expense or depreciate and be confident that the IRS will not be knocking on your door to audit you. They will set-up your books so that you, your banker and the IRS will know where you stand at any given time.

Your accountant should be able to answer your questions about your business. They should be able to provide you with reports in a timely manner and point out to you those areas that need to be looked at. Such items as costs ballooning for feed or labor or a decrease in income from a particular area. Does he have to have horse experience in order to do this? No. He can research how your business compares to other similar businesses and arrive at a conclusion on matters. But if the accountant views your business as a hobby and a way to reduce your taxes from your day job, find another accountant.

Everyone has something to say about lawyers. Good, bad or indifferent. But when you find one that has your best interest in mind, hang on to him. My attorney knew nothing about the horse business when we started, but he knew about contracts, security agreements, about business and their structures, tax issues and estate planning. Over the years, we have built a very good relationship. I trust that he will not advise me about a question I might have without researching it first.

An attorney should be willing to advise you before you jump, to give you a legal opinion on matters and what the end result may be from a judicial standpoint. He should be willing to give a letter of legal opinion on those matters that will help you if the IRS or some other legal authority questions you about your way of doing business. The lawyer should also be available to answer your questions and, if he does not know the answer, to find out for you through research into past case histories and give you a written opinion.

Finding the right attorney for you and your business will take time and some research. It is better for you to have one who has a practice in the area or state where you live. That does not mean an attorney in another state cannot advise you if he is able to practice in your state but sometimes a face to face consultation is more important. A good attorney will save you money and may prevent the possible loss of assets.

Insurance of your business is very important in order to preserve your assets. Here is the one place where you want an expert. Do your research in finding a bloodstock agent who has experience in insuring farms, horses and horse business. True, any insurance agent can write a policy to cover your horse activities. But this is one area where you want your coverage to pay if you or your employees make an error or omission during the course of business, or the principal horses have an injury, become impotent, or dies.

You can ask others in your area who they use as an agent. Good insurance agents are hard to find because of the nature of the horse business. Be truthful with the agent you select. Do not gloss over any incidents that have happened to horses in your care whether those incidents resulted in a lawsuit or settlement or not. You should insure any items that can result in the loss of assets or income. This is one area that it is better to have too much rather than too little.

A qualified veterinarian with extensive equine experience and who is still learning is a must. The way we can treat horses for injuries is rapidly improving. Accidents that used to be life threatening are not necessarily so. His expertise will help you in making decisions regarding your breeding or training operation. If you are boarding for the public, his ability to respond quickly to emergencies and prevent a problem from becoming serious is most important. Take your time and find one who is well qualified before you need him. Get him involved in your business and listen to him. If you don't understand, ask questions until you do. Most vets will tell you everything you need to know in order to make an informed decision.

As you grow your business, you will meet and talk to people with similar interests and businesses. I would urge you to talk to those persons about their business practices, ask questions and be genuinely interested in them. They are a source of information that can help you on a day to day basis. As you attend clinics and other horse related activities, ask those that impress you, if they would mind when you have a question about something, if you could call or email them. I am sure that most will answer in the affirmative.

Do you have to do everything the way they do it? NO! But you can incorporate those practices that may be beneficial to you and your business. If you need to be innovative, be innovative. What works for me may not work for you. You may be more cautious about certain things than I am. But you can take something you learned and tweak it to fit your programs.

If you are an instructor or trainer, take courses on how the other guy is doing it. If you are a breeder, talk to other breeders; take courses on equine management and breeding. Keep up to date on the latest practices whether you use them or not.

How big or small your advisory board is depends on you. It can be three or four or it can be more. The most important thing is that all involved be willing to share information with each other. Those who ask and never give are the ones who suffer. Be innovative. You can usually use some of the information to your advantage if you take time to review it before implementing it. Be tolerant of others, they are learning too. At my advanced years, I still learn from those around me and some are old enough to be my grandchildren.

One last word. From time to time, it may be wise to add or subtract from you advisory board. Only you can decide. An advisory board is good only as long as it has the business in the forefront. If it does not, then changes should be made that will benefit the business and help it achieve its goals.

14

Profit Motive

Profit motive according to the IRS is the intent to make money with your business venture within a reasonable time. The code says that you should have at least two years of profit within seven years. But here is a real piece of news for some. There is nothing in the tax code that says what that profit has to be. It could be $1.00, hopefully it will be much more but at some time it will be very small. That is the nature of this business.

For some, they want to enhance their lives, gain independence, and have control over their future and to enjoy the horse and the lifestyle that accompanies that enjoyment. For others, in the horse industry, they have a substantial primary income; lots of disposable funds and a tax bill that is 40 to 50% of their gross. So, having heard that you can lose lots of money with horses and deduct the expenses, they become involved in horses.

This way of reducing your tax bill is not recommended by me or any of the professionals, (attorneys, accountants, business advisors) I know, for the simple reason that sooner or later, the tax man will want to know how you lost so much money and are still in business. A prudent business owner will want to make a profit in a reasonable amount of time or sell the business venture to someone who thinks that they can make it go or more simply just close the doors.

To have a profit oriented motive does not mean that you can or have to accomplish that in the first year. In fact, you may not be able to accomplish it for a period of years. Depending on what part of the industry you enter, there will be a period of time in which you have little income as you acquire a location to conduct your business, hire and train employees, build improvements, do research on market conditions relating to the business, etc. These items can be capitalized over a minimum period of 60 months after you start the business.

A person that opens a boarding barn or becomes a trainer has a better chance of achieving a profit in a shorter period than a person who wants to build a breeding program involving a particular breed and bloodline achieves. One who opens a feed and tack store or becomes a farrier will be able to show a profit within a few months if they have done the initial steps to opening a business.

If you have done all the things that are necessary to opening a business and it is not going to make a profit for some time, you may want to consult with your accountant about filing a Form 5213 with the IRS at the end of your tax year. The rules are that the business cannot have been operating for more than three years. It will extend the time for a determination by the IRS as to whether your activity is a for-profit or not-for-profit business. This applies to breeding, racing, training or showing horses. The period is extended until the sixth year of the business in these cases. If your business is not any of the above, it will extend the determination until the fourth year of that activity. It will also extend the period that the IRS has to audit your operation as to whether it is a profit making business or not.

Some professionals consider that doing this may red flag your business at the IRS but in this time where the economy is in a state of turmoil, it may give you the needed time to start making a profit. I would urge you not to waste the time gained in hoping that the enterprise will become profitable during that time. An owner should be looking at the changes that are occurring in the marketplace and developing a plan to counter the results of those changes.

I am particularly aware that some disciplines and horse business ventures are still making a profit even in a down economy. Additionally the horse population has expanded by 2 million in the last 10 years increasing the work force necessary to service that growth and the economy surrounding it.

If a business is nearing its third year of being in operation and the expenses are still way ahead of income, the owner should be looking at the business and analyzing what can be improved or changed to reach a profitable year more quickly. They should be looking for ways to increase their customer base, pare costs and overhead, and overhaul their advertising to respond to the current market.

Your location, (urban, suburban, or rural), choice of venture, (breeding, boarding, training, etc.), market conditions for your business in the region or area that your business is located in are factors to be reviewed with your board of advisors.

Market conditions differ greatly from one area to another. Registered working horses at one sale may be $2500 or less and five hundred miles away, the same horse will bring double or triple that price. Show horses are always in a state of flux depending on who is winning with what horse, changes in the breed association rules, (excessive white rule, one registered parent rule, how many ounces in the shoe, length of toe, use of aids (gimmicks), etc.) and the list goes on and on.

Marketing outside of the auction or show arena is important. You should not depend on one avenue of advertising to establish your training, boarding or breeding programs. One must have a realistic advertising budget that will entice the buying public to consider buying a horse from you, having you train a horse, boarding their horses with you or breeding to your stallion.

Your business should be guided towards being profitable from the very beginning. If the sole purpose of the business is to provide you with a way to pursue your favorite horse activity, you may want to reconsider whether you are a business or just a hobbyist looking for a way to deduct your horse expenses from your gross income. Before the IRS determines it for you.

15

Determining Value

I have often had inquiries about how to establish the value of your business. Most of them had a farm or horse facility plus broodmares, stallions and young horses coming up, equipment, tack and other items that were their collateral. But, they couldn't get an operating loan from the bank.

This is not an isolated case but occurs all too frequently. If the horse business is your second income, you can get a loan based on your primary income and credit record. If your primary income is horses, then you have to jump through the hoops that every business goes through.

It is important to realize that your most valuable asset is the facility. The land will increase in value over time. The buildings will depreciate each year but if you improve or add to the existing structures, you can maintain their value for a longer period.

Besides your tax statement each year, you should consider having a real estate appraiser appraise your property before applying for a loan in which the real estate may serve as collateral. The lender will do this for you but in my experience it is better that you have an independent appraiser do this. His agenda will not be to satisfy loan requirements and he will be more realistic in his approach.

Appraisers compare recent sales of similar properties and arrive at a value for the property. Rural properties are harder to appraise because of variables not found in urban areas. If a large area of land is involved, you may find that it is quite a bit cheaper than a five or ten acre property. The buildings used in a horse business are not commonly found in cities and are not a multi-use structure (office, warehouse, etc.) so their value is sometimes understated.

If you are going to use livestock and equipment for collateral for an operating loan, you should have a certified livestock and equipment appraiser do the appraisal. This appraiser should know what the current market prices are in your region and nationally. He should have extensive knowledge of the breed involved in your program and the equipment used in horse operations, some of which is not used in any other business i.e. walkers, saddles, trailers, etc.

What you paid for your horses may not be their true value in the market place. If you have bred and raised them but have not sold many; their value may not be established. What you think they are worth may not be what they will bring when sold in a competitive marketplace. Use of an appraiser gives the lender the opinion of an experienced third party.

The loan officer, unless he has extensive experience with the horse business, will not know what they are worth. In most cases, he will under estimate their worth. If you have an appraisal done before you apply for the loan by an accredited appraiser, the lender will be more likely to grant you a loan for the amount you are seeking.

You should act like a business owner when pursuing funds for your horse business. A lender wants to see your P & L statements, income tax filings for the last 4-5 years, appraisals of your facility, livestock and equipment, business plan and the research you have done. Operating loans are generally for a short period of time and capital improvement loans may be for as long as 30 years.

Be prepared with projections of costs and income for your project that you are seeking funds for. Whether it is a new arena, addition to your breeding program, etc. put it down on paper and include it in your request for funds.

If the lender says that your business is a hobby because you have substantial other income or he wants to grant the loan based on your day job, I would recommend that you look for a lender who will judge your request on its merit. However, you should point out to him that if things go wrong, you have sufficient resources to pay off the loan i.e. your day job.

It is a good idea to talk to more than one lender when seeking funds. Do not overlook sources such as SBA, Farm Credit, credit unions or loan brokers. Other sources, not often thought of, are your insurance agent whose company does farm loans, the Farm Service Agency who serves your area or the Economic Development Department of your state government. Be patient and resourceful when looking for funds; do not accept the first one who offers you the loan. Check current rates and period of the loan. It will vary from lender to lender and you want the best possible rate and period.

Another thing that you will accomplish doing all the above is if the IRS does audit you in the future, you will have the paperwork done to prove your case and a better chance of securing a favorable opinion. You can prove that you are a business with a profit motive supported by appraisals, profit & loss statements and other evidence.

16

So You Want To Be Involved In Horses

Over the years, everybody that applied for employment with me wanted to become a trainer. They wanted to ride horses when what I really needed were stall cleaners, grooms, bookkeepers, groundskeepers, etc.

There are more opportunities for support personnel than trainers. If one can be an accountant, attorney, consultant, groom, groundskeeper, stallion manager, mare manager, veterinary assistant, etc, etc, one will always be able to find employment. A person will not be dependent on one breed or one discipline for employment.

Often I am asked how to get into the horse business. My question in return is to ask what the person is doing now in his 9 to 5 employment. For some reason, people think that you have to be a trainer or own a big horse facility to be in a horse business. The average person can take his skills and education and have a business that involves horses and horse people.

People are constantly searching for attorneys, accountants,

insurance agents, real estate agents, and business consultants to answer their questions and aid in the planning and managing of their horse business. They need landscapers, carpenters, plumbers, leather repairman, and office help to maintain and run the business.

In this age of specialization, I would caution you that it is better to know a little about a variety of jobs and to know one job very well. Why? When one is looking for employment with an employer, if you have knowledge of many things and how they are done, you may be employed even if the position does not involve your area of expertise.

A person who has professional training in any of the previously mentioned fields can increase their income by adding the horse industry to the areas they service. The horse industry is the same as any other business with few exceptions so one can utilize their training in their particular field to not only increase their earning potential but to be involved with horses and that lifestyle.

If one is really dedicated to becoming involved with horses as a trainer, a person must be willing to pay their dues. The community is not closed but the people who make their living with horses know how demanding it is. If you want eight-hour days, forty-hour workweeks and two-week vacations every year, this is not the place for you. If you want to start at the top, that won't happen.

You will clean a lot of stalls, groom many horses, and get to ride some very tough animals before you get to do what you want. And along the way, you will wonder if it is worth it. That is a decision you must make.

On the other hand, if your parents or you have determined that advanced education is needed before you enter the horse industry, I commend you. Too often a person gets caught up in the doing and forgets the planning. If you are a trainer, and a horse injures you, what would you do if that were all you knew? The same applies to the other jobs that we commonly do around horses.

A personal note. When I was training, boarding and breeding, some of my clients asked me what I would do when I retired. They were of the opinion that horses were all that I knew about. That was fine with me because I knew that I could do other things and still be involved with horses. Now they know too.

Many of you have pleasant memories of working with horses when you were young. And now you are older, you have a family, your day job provides you with a comfortable living but----what you really want to do is to be with horses. You want to recapture that feeling you had when you were young. You will buy a horse for your children and then try to relive your experiences through them. Or, you may buy a horse for yourself and then become disenchanted because it is not like the horse you had when you were young. Time changes many things, the past or the future never has any low spots but the reality is that life is full of highs and some lows.

If one would first look at what his current employment entails, then research to see if it can be adjusted to be of use in the horse industry, I think that you would be much more content and happy. A person would have time to develop their horse business while maintaining their current lifestyle with your day job.

There are many opportunities to participate in the industry. A stable owner or trainer would welcome someone to do their billing every month so they can do what they do best. If everything got billed that should be, most of us would make more money than before.

If a person wanted hands on position, you may want to be a groom responsible for the care and grooming of several horses. Don't take offense if the owner of the barn or trainer wants to feed the horses, we just want to know how they are doing. But most of us would rather be on the horse than getting him ready to ride.

The average horse business owner does not know how much trouble they are in until the IRS or the process server shows up at the door. If you have a legal or accounting practice just educating those people will help you and them immensely.

Most horse people are looking for a property to put their horses on or to start their business. A real estate professional who has an interest in horses and takes the time to develop a reputation in the horse community can significantly increase their income.

Almost every occupation and business can be involved in this very exciting and challenging business. The decision is up to you.

17

Preserving Assets

Some of the most important decisions you will make as you progress with your business is how to preserve the assets so your business can go on. We all face hurdles during our life such as the death of one of the principal horses or humans, unfavorable audits or lawsuits, injury to a valuable animal or ourselves. The list goes on and on. Our hope is that our business will prosper and we will be able to leave an estate for our heirs that will provide for them.

Structuring your business as a S corp. or LLC will help do that. Your personal assets are not risk because of unfavorable actions against the business. Owning the land, house and accompanying buildings as an individual and renting or leasing the facility to the business will help do that. When you sell the real property, you can get your exemption on your personal residence and sell the business as a separate entity.

Having an accountant who is aggressive in pursuing every legal deduction is extremely helpful. There are many ways to shelter income that are legal. If you are entitled to use them, do so. Use of Section 179 depreciation can help if you have excess income to protect. Ask your accountant about what is new each year. Sometimes, there are deductions that do not make it into the tax code until after it is printed. Your accountant should know about them. If not, file an amended return. Do not leave any money lying on the table.

Take all the legal deductions. Expense all those items that are necessary to the business, i.e. car expense, repair expense; depreciate every item used, horses, equipment, etc; and ask your accountant if you have any doubt about whether you can expense or depreciate an item.

Above all, pay yourself a living salary. Many of us do not do this. If the business cannot support itself and give us a monetary return, we need to make changes, so that it can do so.

When you are making a profit, shelter it by investing in conventional ways. Money market accounts, stocks, savings accounts, etc. You are building for the future. Pay as much attention to this as to your business.

Hire a good attorney who will answer your questions about the business. Take his advice. It will save you money. He knows about the legality of business better than you do.

An insurance agent who knows about the horse industry and depends on his living from it is a must. He will be genuinely interested in your business and is not afraid of making suggestions on how you can protect your assets by insuring them. You may think that this is an item you do not need or cannot afford. But one lawsuit prevented will pay for all the insurance you will ever need. You should have liability, comprehensive, errors and omissions, mortality insurance on the principal horses and humans, partnership insurance if you have a partnership or syndicate, fire, wind, flood, tornado. Whatever is unique to your part of the world.

An often overlooked way of preserving our assets is that of

dedicated employees. Procuring, training and retaining people who have an interest in the success of your business will make it easier to have a growing business that is successful. It is important that you have a company policy that tells about your business and what its goals are. It should outline the duties of the employee and make him/her feel that they are important to your success.

The last thing is the most important. You must treat your business as your employment. It is your job, not your hobby or something you do in your spare time aside from your day job. If you do not, you will not succeed. If you do not wake up each morning looking forward to your day and enjoying each moment, you should not be involved in the horse industry.

Just one more thought. If you are successful, (and most are that dedicate themselves to the business) you will handle more money that you ever thought possible. Give some thought to how you will spend the 2% that might be left over after you pay the help, IRS, feed bill, etc. Sometimes it is better to not even think of all the money you are accumulating until the end of the year. I've had a few partners who thought that all that money was theirs. It wasn't, just what was left over at the end of year after the taxes were paid. The fact that they got a reasonable paycheck every month didn't count with them. The most that anyone can count on in any successful business is to get a reasonable return on your investment and not have someone else sign your paycheck. Anything else is gravy and should not be taken for granite.

18

Increasing Your Income

Every one of us who has a barn has an arena of some sort that is capable of increasing our income. We only use it during the week and the boarders we have use it in the evenings or on the weekends. We can utilize it to increase our income by putting on a horse show or more aptly a schooling show.

I discovered this when we had a 4H group who used our arena to practice in. The leader approached me about putting on a horse show for the kids, even said that she would do all of the announcements, flyers and ribbons. All we had to do was furnish the arena and get someone to judge the show. One of our customers, who had extensive horse experience, wanted to judge and even did it for free. One hundred and fifty 4H'ers showed up to ride in our arena which was only 60' X 80'. Needless to say, we had to break up the larger classes. We ran two or more smaller classes for each one and then had the winners go against each other for the big win. Much like some of the larger world shows.

Everyone had a good time and so was born a new business for us. Putting on schooling shows for those that wanted to get experience for the breed and larger point earning shows. Some of our participants went on to compete at the national level and did quite well.

We went to a friend who was a trainer and had a larger arena. His arena was mostly used during the week so we approached him about putting on a schooling show once a month. He agreed to our terms of 50% of the net income of the show and we were off and running. We had flyers printed up and posted them at every barn in 50 mile radius. Then we ordered the ribbons from one of the ribbon companies and solicited a judge who was approved by the state horse show association.

I was amazed by the turnout. Over 300 participants of all age groups and levels. We had 4H'ers, kids just wanting to show, adults who wanted the experience and trainers looking for some place to put some time on their young show horses. And the really plus side of this. We got our students some show experience and the boarders got to show their horses.

You should be sure that your insurance will cover you. If it does not, get a rider attached to your policy. You should also post the Limited Liability sign and your entry form should have a release attached to it. Accidents happen.

If you think about this, it is a smart way to keep your arena busy in the slack months. You will create more public exposure to your barn. Your boarders and students are more at ease because the competition is their friends and buddies. And you generate income with little cost.

All horse trainers and stable owners are horse traders at one time or another in their careers. We find a horse that we think has the potential to sell for more than its cost if we put some time on them. Or, one of the boarders or clients leaves without paying the bill and we are stuck with the horse. A word of caution, if you inherit a horse, you should have the owner sign a bill of sale otherwise you may have to pay the owner when you sell the horse. And it will be more than you expected—much more.

You can use this to your advantage, especially if you are just starting out. If you don't have many horses in the barn, you can work on this one and maybe recover your costs and gain customers by having a horse that you have made to show what you can do.

Another way to reduce costs is to partial lease horses to people who want a horse to ride. They pay for part of the board and other costs in return for having a horse that they can ride when he is not doing something else. You should set definite times when the horse is available so they feel a sense of having a horse of their own. If one horse does not work out, you can substitute a different one, who may be more suitable for them.

The other side of this is to ask a boarder if you can use their horse for lessons in return for a reduced rate on their board. You should have a contract that states how often you will use the horse and what the dollar amount is that you will reduce the board. It should include who pays for what, i.e.; vet, farrier, vaccinations, etc. The owner gets free training of the horse and has an animal that may be worth more if they decide to sell it.

In the above examples, one should have a competent attorney draw up the contract and be sure to cover items such as insurance on the horse and rider, when the horse is to be used and what that use shall be. The owner may only want the horse used in certain disciplines and at certain times. They may have other items that they want included.

Empty stalls at certain times of the year can be a problem as they reduce your income while your overhead goes on. If you can rent them out to horse transports that are moving through your area, you can improve your income. Using one of the directories that specialize in listing stopover areas will help you get your name in front of them. You should list your day rate and what the facility has to offer. Do not forget to tell them how far you are from the main highways and how to get there. List your phone number and e-mail address.

National horse transports are always looking for stopovers that are convenient to major highways. You may have to contact them and reduce your rates some but they are an excellent source of additional income. Horse show people who are traveling to the world show are another group who are always looking for convenient layovers. As with any part of your business, you must aggressively market your service to this group.

Market breeders are another source of income for you to consider. They are raising foals to sell at one of the prestigious horse sales in different parts of the country. They may have more than they can handle to get ready for the sale or they may not be set-up to do it. If you have just a few horses in the barn, you can fill the stalls and get these horses ready for the sale ring. It is not any different than getting a show horse ready. You condition them, get them used to being handled, and teach them to stand and all the other things that go along with making a horse out of them.

Another area that is fast developing is that of retirement facilities for older horses. These horses that once were sent to Europe can not do that anymore because of legislation that is being passed nationally and regionally. There is a market for facilities that have lots of unused pasture and turnouts to board these animals. The owners pay a nominal sum for their board and care and you increase your facility's income.

As you progress in the horse industry, you will come to be recognized as an expert especially if you are successful in your endeavors. People will come to you for advice, to have you sell their horse or to get them a new horse. You have spent time and money to learn your business and now you should charge for it.

You should have a price list drawn up for your convenience to refer to. Put down all of the things that you will do for a client and a dollar amount for that service. Some items to consider are commissions to buy or sell a horse, your hourly rate for consultation, how far you are willing to travel in search of a horse or to give advice and anything else that you are going to do for your customers.

You can always increase your income by being aware what is going on in other regions and whether those endeavors will be needed or desired in your area. If they seem to be of benefit to your clientele, then it would be wise to be the first to offer them in your area. It is better to lead the way and reap the rewards than come along in line and just get the left-overs.

Another way of increasing your barn income is to rent the stalls to a trainer or instructor who does not have their own facility. Before doing so, you should write down what you expect of the outside trainer/instructor, what hours they can use your arena, how you are going to be reimbursed for wear and tear of the facility, and who is going to feed and clean the stalls. Items such as insurance, who calls the vet, shoer or owner in case of emergency, will need to be discussed. It is a good idea to have your attorney draw up a contract with all the terms in it and have it signed by the person before you let them move in.

I have rented out stalls to other trainers or instructors over time and have had very few problems. The biggest problem that I have had was that they started thinking they were my sole source of income and acted like they were making the mortgage payments. I learned to address those issues early on and thereby avoided the problem of losing a considerable amount of income when they left in middle of the night taking half of the barn with them. My advice is to address any concerns before you let them in and have a written contract stating all of the terms for their use of the facility.

Another avenue for increasing your income is in your tack room and feed room. We acquire saddles, bridles and other tack over a period of time. We may think we need it to show a particular horse or we just want it. It may have been bought at a tack auction, a tack store close-out or it is something new to us and we have to try it out. We use the item for a period of time and then something else comes along and we hang it on the wall. It just hangs there. But we can turn that around by selling it.

Once people find out that you have tack for sale, they will flock to your door looking for items to buy for their needs. You can find a distributor that will sell to you at wholesale and stock more items that your customers ask for.

We buy hay and grain in quantities in order to get the best price. We can resell those for a profit particularity if there is not a feed store close to us. I buy my concentrates (grain and supplements) from a feed mill that custom mixes them to my specification. Since they are not available at a feed store and my horses do really well, clients and others with horses around me buy those from me. It is the same with hay. I buy in truck and trailer load quantities because I have the room to store them. The person that does not have the room or as many horses will buy small quantities from me. I mark those items up enough to offset the cost of handling and storage plus a small profit.

One of my acquaintances discovered another way to make money. The manufacturers of horse shampoos, conditioners and other items manufacture the same items for human consumption. She approached these manufacturers about handling their human products as well as the horse products. And now she can service her customers with both their equine and personal needs.

The horses in our barn produce a product that we sometimes wish they wouldn't. Manure! The average horse produces about 4000 pounds of this a year. If we have a lot of pasture we can utilize it to fertilize the pastures, up to 4000 pounds per acre per year. Most of us have more horses than we have acreage. The problem is how to get rid of it. I discover this way of getting rid of it when I had a barn that was just down the road from a nursery. I piled it up in a compost pile and twice a year they came and cleared up the pile. Later on, I sold it to a company whose business was making and selling organic fertilizer. Then a person who had a vineyard approached me to buy it. There are many people who want it to use as it is not as nitrogen rich as cattle and chicken manure.

If you have an area with a concrete slab to stack it on so it will compost more easily and is accessible to loaders and trucks, and want to get rid of it, you may want to approach people who may have a need for it and increase your income. We need to always be searching for ways to increase our income and thereby improving our bottom line.

19

Maintaining your Business

As I am starting to write this, we are in very tumultuous times. We are starting to recover from the worst recession since the 30's, fuel prices are up and down, food prices are up and the housing market is plagued by foreclosures, major businesses are trying to hold on by cutting back on production and personnel or going bankrupt. Wages are stagnant and the dollar is trading at par with other currencies.

So, how do you combat this? Let us talk about this in a rational manner and move beyond the war stories that abound at this time. Many horse business owners are struggling to stay afloat, let alone grow their businesses. Having been through this before, though not this bad, I am going to share with you some insights to grow your business in the down side of the economy.

Any recession is bad for all of us but it does not necessarily mean the end of our business. We must budget our expenses more closely than before and work harder to maintain our income. Since horses fall into the recreational column quite often in today's society, along with ATV's, boats, motor homes, etc., horse businesses suffer just like other recreational businesses. But there is one major difference. You can't just put them in the barn and wait until things get better. They have to be fed, sheltered and some routine maintenance is necessary.

There are a multitude of war stories during this time of a severe downturn in the horse market brought about by the closure of the kill plants in the U. S. and the passage of bills by the Congress that limit what you can or can not do with your horses. BUT—there is still a market for horses if you will do several things. This writer has written for several years that this was going to happen and made suggestions about what you should do to prepare for this.

The first thing that you should know is that there is a need for boarding stables, trainers, rescue facilities, retirement farms for aged animals, maybe more so than there has been. Also, there is a need for support personnel and professionals to help the owners of these businesses.

Part of the problem are the groups that have stepped in and created romance stories and myths about the horse in North America. The wild horses that exist in the US today are so far removed from the Conquistador's horses that there is not any resemblance to them in blood or type. The wild horse today is the cast-off of the horses that the early settlers and ranchers did not need or could not use for one reason or the other.

With the fluctuating dollar, apprehension about the downturn of the economy, and the environmental changes in many areas, horse owners are trying to sell, give away or otherwise dispose of their horses.

So, gather up your business plan and your profit and loss statements and let us get started. The first step in maintaining your business is to review your business plan.

Our business plan is our road map for our business. It states what we want to accomplish and our goals, how we are going to do that, when we expect to accomplish those goals, why we think that our service is needed in the area we serve and who we are, our expertise, our facility, our advisors and our employees or independent contractors expertise.

If we have a primary income that is not related to our horse business, we get very complacent about creating a business plan until it is too late. As a consequence, we put not only our horse business at peril but our primary income.

As with all roads, we come upon unexpected road blocks and must take a detour in order to reach our destination. Our industry is a cyclical business. It has its ups and downs depending on the economy, cost of labor, feed, and the bloodlines of the horses involved or the disciplines that are in favor.

We must map out a new route to take us to our destination. To do this, we need to review our current business plan, take a serious look at it and answer these questions. Did we have on rose-colored glasses when we did it? Were our emotions more in control than our brain? Were we in love with a certain animal, breed or discipline and not paying attention to what the marketplace needed or demanded? Were we overly optimistic about our chances of success or did we overstate our expertise? Did we listen to the advice of others, (our advisory team, other people involved in the industry) and take that into consideration in making our decisions?

We have invested time and money into our business, plus a lot of ourselves into this project. Any business owner faces these problems and has to determine the course that will restore them to profitability. So let us begin with our road map (business plan) and plot a way around the road block and back on our way to success and profitability.

We should do some basic research to help in identifying

problems that are impeding our progress. We should ask ourselves, our clients, our advisors and our competition, questions such as; how has the marketplace changed? How is it different than when we began our horse business? Ask your clients, what they want and how you can provide that. Talk to your competitors about what they are doing and why they are doing it. Talk to your accountant and bank about what they feel is going on in the community.

Armed with this information, we need to pull out our profit and loss statements for the last few years and start going through them. We are looking for items that are costing us far more than the return is. We, also, want to identify those items that are producing the most income. You should be looking for the number of horses in the barn, what disciplines are producing the most and the least income, number of employees, taxes among other items.

Most barns do not operate to full capacity for a variety of reasons. Pricing, quality of care, lack of concern for the client and their horse are among the reasons that people often give for not using a particular barn. Other problems that barns have is the lack of qualified help, poor buying of feed, not understanding the requirements of a particular animal, i.e. feeding all animals the same without regard to their work.

Trainers and instructors have similar problems. They get locked into a particular discipline or type of animal and therefore do not have a large enough base to weather the ups and downs of the region they are in. These are correctable but it is important to recognize that they exist and you must be willing to take action to correct them. In order to do that, we have to know what our costs are and what our markup of those costs should be, so that we have a product or service that can be appealing to the public and still provide us with adequate income.

A properly set up accounting program will help identify those areas that need attention. If your books are not set up so that you can determine the number of horses you have boarded or being trained at any time, the number of employees needed to take care of them, you need to do so. You want to be able to know how many horses you have in the barn and what the cost is to keep each one. An average of the cost to keep each horse will help in determining what you should charge to keep the doors open. Don't forget to include items such as water, electricity, taxes, repair expenses, labor, as well as feed, bedding, etc.

Too often, we become single minded about our business. We are successful at a discipline or breeding program and are reluctant to go beyond that point. That is not necessarily a bad thing but we must be objective as well as subjective. We want to grow and expand the business for many reasons, probably one of the most important to many of us, is that we want it to support us and our family, and provide for our retirement.

I recommend that you set up your horse business as an S corporation or limited liability company in order to protect your other assets from exposure to the liability of your horse business. Events happen that we do not have any control of. We are involved with animals that are sometimes unpredictable and/or people who may have exaggerated their experience with the animal. It is very important to remove your personal assets such as your house and land, personal vehicles and other income from the business so if the business has to terminate or is sued, you do not lose everything you own.

As you go over your business plan and P & L statements, you will find those areas that are unprofitable. You should look at their impact on the bottom line and ask some serious questions of yourself. Can they be improved so they contribute to the profitability of the business or should they be terminated? Some will need a little tweaking in order to become profitable while others just do not fit into the greater scheme of things. You should be willing to change and modify your business plan if after a decent interval of time, if it will not help grow the business.

How do you find out which part of your business is earning its way and those that aren't? Get out your handy calculator or have your accountant do it for you. You take your overall gross income divided by the gross income of the individual item. Suppose that your overall gross income is $100k and your boarding income is $35k per year. $35 divided by $100k is 35% of your total income. Do this for each item that you want to track. The more itemized you are, the more likely you are to identify those items that need revising or deleting.

Next you want to track the expenses for those items. It will include electricity, water, taxes, wages as well as feed and bedding. You can find this information in your expenses column of your P & L. Once you have this information, you would take the gross profit and divide by the gross expense for that item. Let us go back to our example. We know that boarding brings in $35k per year and our expenses related to that are $25k per year. 25k divided by 35k gives about a 7% net profit for that item. In order for this to produce the optimum net profit of 33%, we have to reduce our expenses or increase out fees. Using this example, we would like to reduce our expenses by a minimum of $8 thousand a year or increase our fees by $15 thousand. There is no set rule as to what your net profit should be but in order to grow your business and pay yourself a decent wage, it should be about 25 % minimum.

As you go down the list of services your horse businesses offers, you may find one that has a low sales volume but that the profit structure is extremely high. You should examine this further to see if this particular area can be increased and still maintain profitability. The primary objective is to increase your profit by eliminating those services that produce the least income and concentrate on those services that have a healthy profit structure. You should also be aware of the cost of those services.

Efficient turnover of inventory, whether it is services or product, translates into more profit with less cost. You will not always make the right decision in what to add to your business. That is not a bad thing in itself, what is bad is holding on to it instead of terminating it as soon as possible. The wrong service, breeding or training program, or product costs. Do your research before you add a service or product, give it a fair chance to see if it is right and if it is not, get rid of it.

Now, that we have identified the obstacles, we should take steps to remove them so we can move on. Our next job is plotting our new road map to our destination.

We should look for opportunities that will enhance our business. Using our previous research, we have identified those areas or items that are producing greater profit in regard to the total cost. We should take a moment to concentrate on those items and think about how we could incorporate them into our business on a larger scale.

Quite by accident, I discovered that a lot of the excess tack that I had in my tack room could be sold. When we are selling a horse, we usually furnished the saddle and tack that the horse had been used to. People started asking if I wanted to sell the saddle or bridle and bit as well. If you are like me, you are always looking for tack that is comfortable to a particular horse and so we accumulate a variety of bits, bridles, pads and saddles as well as show halters, etc.

The outcome of all this was to start selling tack in addition to boarding and training. We approached some manufacturers of tack, were given a reasonable discount off of retail and were able to mark it up enough to produce a reasonable income from it. From this, we progressed to selling feed as well as tack. We bought hay in truckload quantities and sold it by the bale to those people around us who did not have the space to store large amounts of feed.

We had a feed supplier who made up our grain ration to our specifications and since it was not available anywhere else, we sold that by the sack. All the customer had to do was look at the horses in our barn to know that it worked and the sales made themselves.

Let me share with you another instance of how this can work for you. A young man I know grew up in a horse family. When his father died, he was left with a lot of bills and not enough income to cover them.

His solution was to go to shoeing school at the local university. He graduated with the knowledge of how to shoe the most difficult animals. Then he apprenticed himself to an established farrier and when that person decided to go back to teaching school (his first love), he inherited that list of customers. In his travels to the various barns, he was exposed to some high end horses and their problems.

One of his clients changed their programs and disposed of the horses that they had. He was able to pick up a yearling stud at a very reasonable cost. He showed him moderately, having some success. But the story doesn't end here. The stallion went on to be a superior producer of national quality babies, who won national championships. As result, his business now includes not only his shoeing practice but a breeding and training program as well.

It is simple things like this that too often are overlooked. As horse people, we sometimes become so involved with our primary business that we forget to look around for ways to increase our sales and improve our bottom line.

I have seen some other ways that seem to work out for the people who put them into practice. As with all new things, you should do some research to see if they would be well received in your area.

One of the new services that I have seen recently is to sell memberships to your facility. If you are a breeder, who is looking to expand your market, what could be simpler than to sell a membership to the urban public? Most want their children to have the experience of taking care of a horse without all the initial expense. So for a small yearly fee, you can expose them to the joys of grooming a horse and riding it (if it is broke) under your supervision.

You should have a contract stating when, where and how the membership works. You don't want them to be wandering in at all times of the day and night. Define when they can see the horse or horses and what they can do. You should not let the activity be unattended at any time and that should be in the contract.

A release of liability is needed. Be sure they understand it and have a parent sign it. If anyone else wants to sign it, say no. If you don't have a parent or guardian, you may lose the farm should someone be injured.

The advantages are; you create additional income, you create a market for your horses and the publicity you receive will help you create a market presence. The disadvantages are minimal if you are diligent in preparing the client and making sure that they understand what is expected of them.

With all the excess animals that are being released on public lands or just turned loose, there could be an opportunity for the person with empty stalls or land. Contacting your local animal control or humane society would be the first step. You should have a presentation that shows what you have available, what you provide, that you have resources to do this, and what it will cost them. Don't forget the horse owner who has a favorite horse but can't afford a large monthly board bill but can afford to pasture board the horse for in indefinite period of time. Once they see that their horse will be taken care of on a daily basis but with less cost to them, they will be willing to board their horse. And they will tell their friends about you and your services.

The closure of the kill plants in the US brings about an opportunity that has not been thought of in the past by some owners. There are many serviceable animals that can not be disposed of as in the past. If you set up as a non-profit rescue, you can help these animals find new homes. By adding value to these animals and finding them proper homes where they are valued. You would also be able to apply for grants offered by the various organizations to save these horses.

There are different types of businesses in certain parts of the country that can be adapted to your area. One needs to be aware of these opportunities, either by exploring them in person or through research.

In the central part of the nation, there are organized trail rides that have 3000 to 5000 participants at a time. They are set up to furnish stabling, food for rider and horse, and personnel that lead each group on a three to eight hour ride each day. They produce a horse show for the participants, a sale, so the participants can sell their horse if they wish, cattle roundups, evening rides and the list goes on and on.

The riders come from all over the US to do this. They stay

a week or a few days. The land used is a combination of private and public land. There are some restrictions on the public lands but by developing a responsible use of that land, there are not any major problems.

It provides the recreational rider a dream vacation, being with others who share their love of the outdoors and horses. In most parts of the country, it has wilderness on trails. It is also an alternative to the dude ranch experience by letting them use their own horse and equipment limiting some of the liability to the seasonal limitations but it fulfills the dream of riding your horse in the business.

Another area that is rapidly coming to the forefront is the Federal and State government's use of sub-contractors to manage and develop campgrounds and state parks. The public who uses these facilities are demanding better accommodations and getting them. Knowledgeable people are being sought to manage these projects and maintain them.

There are many other endeavors that produce a good income for the owners at a reasonable cost. One should always be looking for ways to improve their service to the horse owning public in their area.

Another good thing that is going to happen, as we recover from this downturn in the economy, is that there will be incentives offered to those businesses that will provide employment to the region that they are in. Most states have some sort of development funds available to those that will provide good jobs and steady employment.

To find out about these funds and other legislation affecting the horse industry, you need to use your board of advisers. Each has a special expertise that can be used to your benefit if you will take advantage of it. Ask questions of them, read the various publications dealing with the horse industry, join those organizations that are involved in the horse industry as well as those that deal with your particular activities. Be inquisitive. You attend clinics to learn to be better horse trainers and you should do the same about your business. You will be better able to deal with the business aspects of your endeavor if you know how to read your profit and loss statement and be able to identify trouble areas just as you learn to be a better horse person.

I have always pointed out that you need more than talent to succeed in the horse industry. The complexity of running a successful business requires that you have some knowledge about the different phases of your business. If you are a trainer, boarding stable, farrier or any of the other employment areas that we have in this industry, you need some rudimentary knowledge of accounting, marketing, etc. so that you are aware of what is happening in your business and whether it is growing or is stagnant.

If you are like many of us, you hold a day job to support your horse addiction. Your employer probably offers clinics or seminars or a chance to attend various courses that will improve your abilities and increase your productivity on the job. It is a win-win situation for both of you. You become more valuable to the company and the company has a long term employee. You can improve your horse business by doing the same. You attend clinics that teach you to be a better trainer or horseperson. You should attend clinics or classes that make you a better business person.

Various community colleges throughout the nation have a small business development program with a wide variety of classes offered. You can look into SBA development loans, accounting programs, marketing programs, mentor programs, web design and many more. The people giving them are experts in their field and their expertise is invaluable to the small business owner.

In this age of electronic technology, we communicate with each other via the internet, sell horses to people outside of our region or nation, import semen from different states or nations by using this media. You can further your education by using the internet. There are all sorts of classes offered online that will help you enhance your business and your resume. You will naturally gravitate towards those classes that you think will enhance your horse knowledge but you should be willing to take some of the more traditional courses too. A well rounded background will give you a better chance at succeeding in your chosen endeavor.

You will at some time in the development of your business need access to capital in order to grow it. While the Small Business Administration, as a rule, does not make direct loans, it does make guaranties on those loans. The Farm Service Agency and the Farm Credit Administration do make loans to agriculture enterprises. The time to find out if either of those agencies can be of help to you is before you need them. They have classes and seminars available to the farm public about what they can do to help them. They have staff that will mentor you about your particular business.

Any education that you get, even if you think that it will not be of any help, will broaden your experience. There is the very real possibility that you may be injured at sometime and not be able to pursue the career with horses that you planned. However, if you have a broad experience behind you, you can find employment in the industry that will still keep you involved with the horse industry. There is always a demand for support personnel in this industry.

Many of us are uncomfortable having to sign our own paychecks. We look for the security that working for someone else brings. We go to work for a recognized farm or trainer. We are comfortable with being the person that handles the day to day routine that goes on in a horse business. Whether it is handling the horses, starting colts, handling stallions and mares or just doing the paperwork that is required. We are happy just to be around the animal we love and knowing that we are contributing to the industry.

If you are lucky enough to find out what really motivates you early on, good for you. Most of us stumble around a bit before we come upon a job that turns us on and that we enjoy working at. I have seen many who thought that they wanted to be a trainer. Once they found out that it was long hours and little pay to begin with, they decide to find another line of employment.

There are many opportunities for those who have other occupations. There is a need for legal advice, accounting advice, what should be insured, marketing advice, etc. Those of us involved in the day to day routine of caring and training the animal have neither the knowledge or desire to learn all the business aspects of the business. We are too busy running the barn and keeping everyone happy.

Another area that needs help is with the landscaping and upkeep of the grounds. While we may be aware of what needs to be done, we simply do not have the time to do it. I appreciated the mothers of my students who did those things while I was teaching their children how to ride and show the horse.

The end result of this is that it doesn't matter what you have learned, there is always an opportunity to learn something else and improve your previous knowledge. While at the time, you are learning the new skill, it may just be for the reason that you are interested in learning how it works or what it is about, later on you may have the opportunity to put that knowledge to work. The most important lesson that you will learn is if you don't know the answer, you will know where to look for it.

All businesses must develop a demand for their product or service. Not doing so spells doom for that business. Every opportunity should be taken to make the buying public aware of your business. Every time that you are in a situation where you are expected to contribute to the conversation, you should be telling people about what you do.

Don't brag but people want to know what it is that you do and if you are successful at it. Tell them. Invite them to tour your facility and see what it is you do. Make arrangements for them to do so.

At some point in your career, you will be looked upon as a go-to person by your peers and those that are your clients and employees. When this happens, accept it with humility and be willing to share your knowledge. Most of the people in this business who shaped the person I am today did so freely and without reservations.

20

Boarding Horses as a Business

During my life in the horse industry, I have had several inquiries and comments about running a boarding facility. Operating a boarding stable can be a rewarding and gratifying way to earn a living in the horse industry. The knowledge that you must have to manage a profitable business in today's world is of paramount importance. I recommend that you have some knowledge of how to run a business. It is important that one knows how to read a profit and loss statement and a balance sheet. Otherwise, you will wake up one morning to find that you must sell your dream or go bankrupt. One can be competitive and still make a profit. The fact that the competition charges less may not be a good gauge of what you should charge. They are not the same as your facility.

Most business operate on a gross profit ratio of 25 to 33 percent or more depending on the location and what the facility has to offer. The expectation is that after all the expenses are paid they will have a net profit of 2 to 3 percent. The mark-up of goods necessary to achieve this should be 33-1/3 to 50 percent. It can be more, it should not be less.

In order to determine what you should charge for your services, you should have the costs of all products and overhead available. Feed, bedding, water, electricity and labor are items that are expenses. You should also allow for vacancies and the cost of acquisition in your planning.

Acquisition is the buying or renting of a facility. Some facilities have residences where owners and other personnel live. A personal residence may or may not be involved in the business. If it has an area that is devoted exclusively to the business, rent for that area should be included in your cost of operation.

Vacancies occur for a variety of reasons. You should assume that at certain times of the year you will have fewer boarders than at other times. While the expenses for feed and bedding will go down during these periods, lights, water, labor and acquisition costs will be the same. Your mark-up of goods must take this into account so you can attain your desired net profit at the end of your fiscal year.

Labor is another area with which we must deal. Employees, whether they are paid a wage or an exchange of services must be included in your cost projections. Horses are known to be labor intensive. We must ascertain the number of work-hours involved in the operation. Even if all the labor is performed by family members, they should be paid a competitive wage and that should be included in your costs.

One of the obstacles that first time stable operators face is the tremendous demand on their time. If they have been used to a 40 hour work week, they will have some difficulty adjusting to a 60 to 80 hour week. The phone ringing at 1 a.m., or a client knocking at your door at 10 p.m. to tell you of some problem, can seriously interfere with your social or family life. You start realize that you have a lot in common with other professional people. The up side of this is that you get to meet and help some wonderful people.

From a practical point of view, a small facility may be fine for a family operation but may be unsuitable for a profit motivated business. There are a specific number of stalls at a certain price you must have in order to make a profit. There is no magic formula to arrive at the optimum number for your operation. It should be in correlation to the dollar volume needed to meet all expenses and produce a profit.

It is important to know about local, county and state zoning laws for the area in which you have your barn. In recent years, as suburban areas have become more populated, a number of laws have been passed controlling the number of animal units per acre, waste disposal and noise abatement. One should be prepared to deal with these issues as they arise. A little forethought and consultation with an attorney, who has a background in land use law and agriculture, will prevent problems from arising needlessly.

In this business, unforeseen problems are a matter of course. Whenever one deals with an animal that is sometimes unpredictable in their behavior, one must assume that something will happen. Usually when you don't expect it. The stress and pressure of the business takes it toll on everyone. Being able to cope with stress is a commendable quality that one should strive to achieve.

You should strive to learn of any new practices or laws that may affect your business. Any education, whether it is horse related or not, that will help you improve your business and expertise at running that business should be seriously considered. Constant improvement and innovation will greatly increase your business's success.

21

Standing a Stallion

An owner, who had among his many businesses, a barn full of young, untrained stallions, hired a young trainer. There was constant screaming and banging of stall walls in the barn, day and night. The owner had to go on a business trip but before leaving he instructed the trainer that he wanted something done about all the noise in the barn. When he returned, he went to the barn and it was quiet and peaceful. He complimented the trainer on doing a good job and asked how he did it. The trainer replied, "You now have 18 geldings and just two studs in the barn."

I can tell you that during the time you are involved with horses that one day you will see a stallion or raise one that you think will be THE ONE!! All of us have a problem gelding what we think may turn out to be our dream stallion. I know I have. The colt would be by super stud or out of super producer and I would put off gelding him. But in the end, when they did not prove out in the ring or in the breeding shed, I gelded them and made useful horses out of them.

The advantage of gelding most stallions is that you can sell them for more money than if they were a stud. The market for good well-broke saddle horses continues to be good, no matter where you live. The same market will sell stallions for very low prices unless they are broke, have a good disposition and some sort of record. Even then, they will not bring what they should.

Every year as I look at the stallion issues of the horse magazines, I wonder what happened to all the stallions that were advertised last year and never show up again. Are they geldings or is the owner simply breeding his own mares? Are the resulting foals of value or something that does not bring enough money to pay for the upkeep and maintenance of the stallion and his mares?

When considering whether to keep a colt for a stallion prospect, one should be aware of many things in making their decision. Pedigree, conformation, sire and dam are just a few. Pedigree is important. Is the sire a producer of foals that can perform or work well under saddle? Has the dam produced superior foals before?

A stallion that does not have any superior ancestors closer than the second generation should be inspected more closely than one who does. Looking beyond the sire and dam is not as important because the second generation only contributes 25% of the genetics to the foal. Going further back is even less important as the percentages that contribute to the foal drop dramatically

The sire should be of superior quality, producing foals out of a variety of mares that are better than the sire or dam. The dam should be capable of producing outstanding foals when bred to variety of stallions. If they are not doing this, you should think carefully about whether it will pay to raise a foal out of them.

Conformation ranks high. Is the individual representative of the breed? Does he have conformation faults that impair his ability to perform? Will he pass these faults on? If he can not do his job, whether under saddle or in the arena, you should geld him.

Behind every stallion that makes a contribution to his breed is a dedicated owner, who makes every effort to promote the stallion. He has qualified personnel train and/or show the horse. He seeks out the best mares to breed to him and is willing to make allowances in order to obtain those mares to breed. His advertising program is consistent and continues over an extended period of time. He utilizes Stallion Service Auctions and futurities to promote the foals. He has an Internet site that advertises the stallion and his foals. The stallion owner realizes that unless the stallion's name is in front the horse buying public all the time that he will not accomplish his goal of making a profit from the stallion and his get.

If one is not willing to devote time, effort and money to the promotion of a stallion, he may want to consider using an outside stallion. If he wants to produce foals that bring a reasonable return, he may want to breed those mares to a stallion that is being consistently promoted.

Gelding a colt may pay off as many registries are encouraging their members to geld their horse colts. They offer sweepstakes that are for geldings only. Some breeders offer a free breeding if you geld the colt that was sired by a stallion that they own.

Ranchers know from experience that a gelding makes a better horse to work stock on the range. They are relatively calm, cool and collected because their hormonal problem has been removed. They can sell those horses for more money than a beat-up stud or an unbroken mare.

In this day of shipped or frozen semen, mare owners have a wider choice of who they can breed their mare to. They are able to select the best stallion from a range of available horses for about what it would cost to breed to a stallion in their backyard.

As the mare to stallion ratio drops for unimpressive stallions, (those without a pedigree, show record, or progeny that do something notable), keeping a stallion becomes less important to the average horse owner. Stallion owners should be really objective about each prospective stallion and if he does not measure up, geld him before it becomes a problem. You will have an excellent gelding without all the problems of stallion.

For whatever reason, stallion owners seem to believe that if they own a stallion, people will automatically breed to him because he is *there*. What often happens is the stallion owners' breed to the mares they own or to their friends or neighbor's mares, and as a result, their stallion never reaches his full potential. In this time, where we have cooled or frozen semen available to mare owners throughout the world, you must actively promote your stallion at all times.

Here are a few things you can do to promote your stallion. You can be successful with your breeding programs and horse business if you do some planning followed by aggressive action.

1. Have a reputable pedigree service draw up a pedigree with a six generation background check.

This will establish what the stallion has done and what his sire, dam, grandsires and grandams have done. For a relatively inexpensive sum, you receive valuable information to give to potential customers and to use in your promotional campaign. Your customers will be impressed by your professionalism and the third party (pedigree service) will lend credibility to your statements about your horse, his background and/or progeny. You can do this on your own using the breed association and their data base but it is time consuming and you have to be a graphic artist in order to create an appealing pedigree.

2. It is important to be competitive and truthful about your fees.

If you set your fees based on what someone else charges and not on what your particular animal is worth, you will miss potential customers. If your stallion has the same pedigree, show record and production, and stands in the same area as another stallion, use him as a guide. If not, it would be beneficial to find a stallion of similar type, pedigree, show record and production record to use as a reference in setting the fee. Remember that a reasonable fee is better than one too high or too low. You want mare owners to consider your stallion for their breeding programs.

My theory has always been that it not what the stud fee is, but how many mares you breed each year. If you look at any top ten list of sires, you will find that the more foals you have on the ground, the more likely you are to have progeny who performing in one or more areas.

3. Breed any mare to a stallion at the same fee whether she is registered or not, or of the same breed or not.

You just never know what is going to happen and you cannot afford to lose the chance to breed the next world champion.

4. You must do some form of advertising on a consistent basis if you want to get mare owners to breed to your horse.

You should use as many different types of advertising as you can and still maintain your budget. Many of the magazines offer a directory or business card section at a reasonable fee. If you use this in your off season, you will gain some name recognition that will be invaluable during your breeding season. Pictorial ads are more likely to attract attention than word ads.

You must have a presentable photo of your stallion that shows his good qualities. A good disposition is desirable but it will not show up in a photograph. A photo must have a passive background even if the animal is in motion. You want potential customers to focus on your stallion, read the brief description about him and then pick up the phone and call for appointment to see him. Your description should be aimed at those who you feel will be the most likely to breed to your stallion based on his pedigree, show record, or progeny. Keep it to the point. Excess verbiage does not get read.

5.   Promotion of your stallion should include press releases, in addition to the more accepted ways of advertising.

Everyone knows that they should advertise the stallion if they want to get outside mares to breed. So, they get a web site and figure everyone will see it and it was cheap, right? But, there are thousands of sites just like yours and the people that may be interested can't even find yours without hours of cruising the web. The way to alleviate this problem is to use the print media to your advantage to get your web address to the public.

Some print advertising should be in regional or national magazines depending on your budget. Local classifieds should also be used. Every print ad should have your web site address and e-mail address as well as your phone number, mailing address, etc. You will increase your likelihood of getting mares to breed immensely.

Too often we become so engrossed in advertising that we pass over opportunities to get our name and stallion before the public for free. One should make it a policy to inform all newspapers, TV and radio stations in your area when you have an event, such as an open barn, when your horses win at a horse show, or when you have out of area guests viewing your horses and facility. Doing this simple inexpensive thing will help your stallion and farm gain recognition in your community.

6. Presentation of the stallion and his surroundings to potential breeders must be appealing and professional.

The stallion should be clipped and groomed before the mare owner sees him. It is a good policy to always present the stallion in a show halter, not a turnout halter. The area where you show your stallion to the customer should be well lighted and free of distractions. Owners will want to know where their mare will be kept and what she will be fed. Have a stall and the breeding area ready to show them.

I cannot emphasize enough the importance of presenting your stallion and your stable in your best professional manner. Potential customers want to see a well groomed, physically fit animal in neat, well maintained surroundings. You do not have to have white fences, but you do have to have a facility that is kept up with safe fences and well-maintained stalls, arenas, and breeding areas.

All of the above will improve your potential to breed mares to your stallion, but it is important to do a follow-up on every inquiry you get. Formulate a plan where you call, write a thank you, or otherwise acknowledge every inquiry. Call backs are important to let people know that you are interested in them and their animals. It will produce business for you even if they do not breed to your stallion this year.

Donations of a breeding to stallion service auctions are another way to get your stallion and his progeny in front of the public. You may have to purchase the breeding yourself but it is advertising. Choose the best mare in your program and hope that the resulting foal will be all that you hope for.

My best experiences have been with open houses or barns or whatever you want to call them. The mare owner gets to come and see your facility and the stallion in his surroundings. It is to your advantage to be able to control the presentation and you have all the time in the world to answer questions, to deal with criticism of your horse and to show mare owners your horse husbandry. You are on your playground and nobody can interrupt your presentation.

7. Probably the most important form of stallion promotion is a pregnant mare and a live foal.

Whether you are doing live cover, AI, shipping semen (cooled or frozen), be honest with the mare owner about your stud's conception rate While 100% conception rates are conceivable, not all stallions achieve that for many different reasons. . Some stallion's semen does not ship well when it is cooled or frozen. Sometimes, the mare is the problem or the vet technician is not as competent as they should be. At the start of the breeding season, the sperm is less viable. You can put the stallion under lights (16 hours a day) sixty days before you breed the first mare and you will increase your chances of getting her in foal. If you offer a return breeding, state the conditions in your breeding contract. But be ready to make exceptions, things happen that we do not have control of.

From a business standpoint, if you want to impress the government, your banker, your accountant or your attorney, it makes sense to advertise your stallion and his progeny. It shows that you are serious about being in the horse business and you are creating a market demand for your product.

Your advertising is a deductible expense. If you have a photographer do the pictures, an ad agency create the layout or place the ads for you, that is an expense that you can deduct. Most magazines have a person who can create the ad with your photos and information at little or no cost to you, just the cost of the ad itself.

Advertising should have a budget amount each year. If you are promoting an unproven or little used stallion, you are going to want to have a bigger budget than if he is a proven stud with progeny on the ground that is competing.

You should also track your ads to see which ones are read and responded to. When someone inquires about your stallion, ask them where they saw the ad or heard about the horse. Record the information so you can make a knowledgeable decision about which media to use and how often. Strategically placed ads are less costly than the shotgun approach to advertising.

22

Choosing a Stallion

Breeding season is fast approaching and you have foal fever. Many of us are looking at stallion advertisements and wondering which stallion will give us the foal that will be everything that we want and still be saleable if we have to or want to. We have many choices in our modern day world. We can breed to almost any stallion we want because of the availability of cooled or frozen semen. We can produce as many foals as we want out of our best mare due in large part to embryo transplants and multiple registrations.

Before deciding on which stallion, we should do some research on the mare and the stallion in order to arrive at our decision. The pedigree of the animals involved should be examined. Are they closely related or are they an outcross? Inbreeding has been practiced for some time in order to produce a more uniform animal in type, disposition, color, height, etc. The breeder is reducing the gene pool and hopefully producing horses that are the same in type. Many well known breeders have gone this route and been quite successful. The down side is that we have created several genetic mutations that are troublesome to deal with and shorten the useful life of the animals involved.

Crossing two different bloodlines has produced some outstanding individuals. The term that I use is hybrid vigor although that is incorrect because I am not crossing different breeds in order to achieve this. The breeder in this case crosses two totally unrelated bloodlines and the resulting foal is superior to the parents and its ancestors. Achieving this 'nick' is time consuming and may take time to arrive at the desired cross. A shortcut is to study pedigrees to determine what outcrosses have produced a superior individual and use it as a guide.

The stallion's progeny record should be perused to determine which crosses have produced outstanding individuals. While we are looking at the progeny records, we will want consider the number of progeny produced, bloodlines of the dams and whether they are producers of outstanding foals. The ratio of performers to progeny produced is important. You may have a stallion with a low number of total progeny but a high number of performers. That could mean that he has not been promoted or that he has never stood to the public before or any of number of reasons.

The stallion's performance record should be examined to see what he has done. His sire and dam's produce and performance records should be looked at. Beyond that, the ancestors contribute 12 1/2% or less to the mix. From my standpoint, they become less relevant to the resulting foal than the immediate ancestors do. From the standpoint of salability of the foal, a sire with performance credentials is important, because basically you are selling the potential of the foal.

This brings us to a point that I think many people overlook. It costs money to maintain a mare to raise a foal. Even if the stud fee costs you nothing, you still have to feed and take care of your mare. At some point in time, you may have to sell the foal. If the selling price is below what the stud fee, the cost of maintaining the mare and raising the foal is, then maybe you should not have bred the mare. At least to that particular stallion.

The dam of your foal is important if you are trying to produce an outstanding animal. The things that you look for in a stallion, (conformation, pedigree, performance and progeny record) should be present in the mare. One trait that I look for in a mare is disposition. It is my experience that if the mare is a witch, the foal will be too. There is a lot of conversation about this and people want the stallion to have an excellent disposition but it is the mare that raises the foal and passes on her external traits to it.

A mare should have some training before she is made into a broodmare. Riding the mare and finding out what capabilities she has under saddle will help determine later what type of stallion you may want to consider. Every horse should have a job besides being a stallion or broodmare. You may have to sell them at some time and the new owners may want to ride or show them, not breed them.

Breeding horses should be done to fill a market need for the type of horse that you are breeding for. Whether you sell the foal or not, one should have a goal in mind for the result, other than babies are cute or you want to give your children the experience of raising a foal.

Any person who decides to stand a stallion or breed a mare should have a goal in mind before they begin. They should be objective about the animal recognizing its bad points as well as the good points. Thorough research into the horse's background, (pedigree, progeny, performance), should be done before the decision to breed is made.

You should recognize that even with all your research that the result may not be what you want. If the foal is not an improvement on his parents, a person should geld him, if it is a stallion or make sure that it is never bred, if it is a filly.

As it becomes more difficult to sell less desirable animals, one should strive to produce animals that will bring enough money to break-even on the costs. The horseperson, who makes part of their living breeding and selling, realizes this. The recreational breeder should observe the same rules for producing saleable horses, instead of flooding the market with less desirable horses.

In the spring when it is nearing time for mares to foal and while I think that everyone enjoys this time, the time to market those foals was before they were born. We are going to look at why some breeders get more money for their horses than others do in this time of market adjustment.

While researching the current horse market, I found that some breeders were getting $5000 up to $30,000+ for weanlings. The sires of these weanlings were not what one would call a leading sire but they did have one thing in common. They were sons of producing sires who had achieved a record, both in the show pen and/or as a sire.

These stallions had been bred to mares carrying bloodlines that had been proven to cross well with the stallion's breeding. What was produced was foals that commanded good prices and were what today buyers are were looking for. Even in a down market, one can be successful if you do your homework. You should be aware of what is hot in your particular breed and try to incorporate that breeding into your program.

What you want to produce with your breeding program are foals that will sell at weanling or shortly thereafter. You want them to bring prices that will pay for the stud fee, mare upkeep and a profit. If you can't do those things, then perhaps you might want to sit down with your advisors and seriously discuss your program and the market.

Finding the right stallion at a reasonable fee can be a task that seems to be impossible, but there are many ways to accomplish it. First, one must find out what bloodlines are bringing the most money on a national scale. A study of horse sales results is important. What is hot in one area may not be in another. With the advent of the Internet, we have a much wider area to sell our foals to.

Once you have identified the stallions whose produce are selling in the market range that you want to sell your foals for, you might want to find a stallion that is for sale and purchase him. You can breed your mares and perhaps some outside mares. You can depreciate the stallion over time and expense his feed and training.

If the stallion's purchase price is more than you are willing to pay, you may want to either buy him with partners or a syndicate. You can still take depreciation and expenses but it will depend on how big a share you have in the stallion on how much you can depreciate and expense.

You can breed your mares to an outside stallion. You can pick and choose which stallion you want to breed to which mare. You can pick the best cross for each mare. Your only expense is the stud fee and mare care over the gestation period. You also can breed to the sons of the leading sires for less than the fee is for their sire.

One of the ways of breeding to top stallions is to buy their service through a Stallion Service Auction. There are SSA's in every state and most horse organizations use them as a way to generate money and interest in their members' horses. Whether you show or not, you can pick up a breeding to these stallions usually by joining the organization putting it on and submitting a bid on the stallion you wish to breed to.

In recent months, I have found listed in SSA's a four time

world champion for an opening bid of $350 plus chute fee and shipping, also a leading sire whose fee was available for half price and the list goes on. Of course, if someone bids more than you do, it may cost you more. Some stallion auctions state that you have to be there in person and some you don't.

The foals produced by these stallions should more than recover the cost of producing them. Since what you have to sell are foals with the potential to become winners or to become good using horses, you have enlarged your market area beyond your region.

An old-timer, who dealt with horses with more success than I could ever attain, once told me that when you are selling young horses, what you are really selling is the smell of the bacon frying in the pan. It may be underdone or overdone but the smell makes your mouth water. What you want to produce are young horses that have the 'smell of bacon frying in the pan'. The potential to do something will bring the buyers to your door.

I know that not everyone wants to sell the foals out of that favorite mare that has become part of family. I, also, know that sooner or later, for one reason or the other, most of the foals, at some point in time, will be put up for sale. I see them at auction sales across the country. I talk to the owners who complain about the low prices and how the buyers don't know a good horse when they see one.

And it boils down to this, when I or the other guy looks at the background, conformation and condition of these animals, we have difficulty in trying to fit them into our programs whether it be breeding, as potential show horses or just horses that our clients will be interested in.

If you are going to breed that mare, choose your stallion carefully. If you are going to breed that stallion, be sure that you can sell what he sires.

23

Getting your Mare
Ready to Breed

A new truck and trailer pulled into the barn and I could hear horses moving around inside. The owner came around to let the mare out, all the time telling me how excited they were about breeding the mare and what they were going to do with the resultant foal. Out stepped this mare with a baby doll head, willowy neck, tremendous hip and—feet that had not been taken care of for months, 200 pounds underweight, hadn't been wormed or had her vaccinations in who knows how long. To top it all off the mare was an aged animal with a sunken anus and the owner had not had a pre-breeding exam done. Unfortunately, this happens more frequently than we wish. Here is what you can do to assure a happy ending to this story.

Before you book a mare to a stallion, you should have breeding exam done, preferably in the fall before you plan to breed. Even if she has had a live foal this year. It is the best way to tell whether the mare is breedable or not. You can find out whether she is ovulating, will need a hymen stretched if she is a maiden mare or a caslick's after being bred if she is an older mare. You can have a general physical done at the same time to determine if she has any other problems that will affect her being a mother. An ultrasound can map the uterus to find any growths that may affect her being able to conceive. This is the time to find out if she will have to be lavaged before and after breeding.

A month before you are going to breed her, you should worm and bring her up-to-date on her shots. It is also the time to have her feet done. You don't have to put shoes on, but she does need to have her feet trimmed.

I like my mare to be in a thrifty condition going into breeding season. Not too fat or thin, just in a good solid frame. I will start them on a light program sixty to ninety days before I plan to breed them. I want them to think that spring has arrived so they get 16 hours of light a day. You don't have to blanket them unless you want to. You can start a ration that will add a little weight to them along with a vitamin and mineral supplement. The most important part is to feed lots of good green roughage with the concentrates and supplements to keep your mare's fertility up and to produce a healthy foal.

Virgin mares and older mares can be put in foal as easily as any other mare. You just need to take the time and effort to get them in condition and keep them that way. What often happens is that you will spend the time and money to get them pregnant and then just turn them out until it is time for them to foal. You need to maintain that condition until 90 days before foaling. At that time you should start increasing their feed so they can keep their condition as this is the time that the foal really starts growing. About 45 to 30 days before foaling, worm and bring them up to date on their shots.

Virgin mares may have an intact hymen that needs to be

stretched before breeding. Your vet can do this for you when he does the pre-breeding exam. Older mares need an exam before breeding especially if they did not have a foal last year. Over time the muscles around the vagina loosen and may allow contaminants to enter the uterus. Often you can lavage the mare before breeding and again after breeding and get her in foal. A simple uterine culture will tell you whether you have to do this. On my older mares, I want them to have a live foal every year. I keep them well-fed and to date on their health care. It is when we allow them not to have foal for several years that we run into problems.

There is nothing that I know of as rewarding as having a good healthy foal out a good mare who is an excellent mother. I have never understood why owners will make a broodmare out of an animal that can't be ridden or handled in a safe manner. If the mare is moody, witchy, or hard to ride, the owner will breed her to a so-so stallion and sell her as a broodmare. The end result is always an animal that has the same characteristics as his parents. If you absolutely have to have a foal, use the best mares you have. Breeding less than desirable mares to stallions is, in my opinion, a waste of time and money.

Another problem I have with mares is that too many of them are bred as two year olds and beyond being halter broke that is all that is ever done with them. I was taught that it is better to let them mature and to put a little or a lot of training on them. You will have a better idea what they are capable of and if you have to sell them, you can get a better price for them.

Many of my best broodmares were five or six years old before I ever thought of breeding them. Some were used on the ranch and some went to the show pen. When I did decide to breed them, I didn't have to worry about getting hurt as they had been there and done that. They were used to being handled and were more or less thoroughly desensitized. I could hobble them if I was doing live cover or give them a mild tranquilizer if I was doing A-I and they would not object. They were used to other horses being around them and being bumped and shoved around and were used to human contact.

Another plus to this is I knew what they were capable of under saddle and an idea of what they might produce when bred to a certain stud. It did not always work out but at least I had a starting point to work from. Little things like that will help you produce saleable foals. And that is the point of breeding horses, isn't it?

24

Reality

I lost a mare recently to the complications of colic. She was pregnant. The unborn foal was by a nationally ranked stallion and my futurity baby for the year. I am pragmatic about the setback and the loss of a good well-bred horse but that doesn't mean that I am not saddened by the event.

In this business of horses, we often lose horses because of things that we don't have any control of. And we lose horses for a variety of other reasons that we can control and don't. In the news that I get on a daily basis from around the world are stories of barn fires, starvation, and assorted cruelty by the use of drugs, infliction of pain and other things.

In my view of the business, one should not produce more than he can afford to feed and maintain. Acquiring large numbers of animals, no matter how cheaply, does not make sense if one can not sell them or their produce at a profit.

I know that the pleasure rider, whose day job provides for the horse as well as the family. owns the majority of horses. But there is a segment of this industry, where people acquire horses just to acquire horses.

Two recent cases involved large numbers of horses. One case involved 131 horses in the Midwest and the other involved 87 horses in a Mountain state. In the Midwest state, we had a mild winter. In some areas, the animals had enough graze not to demand much supplementary feeding. However, running large numbers on acreage without some supplementing is not recommended. In the other case, the 87 horses were on a 77-acre farm, in a state where the winters are never that mild and feeding is taken as a matter of course.

Why is it that people buy horses at a low cost and immediately think that they can sell them for more money? In order to market that animal, one must do something to add value. Added value can be feeding and training, breeding to a good stallion, or fattening up and selling them to Europe.

If you are simply buying in order to say you have x number of horses, you are not doing justice to the horse or you. It is like building a 150' by 250' arena when a sixty-foot round pen will do.

People buy horses to keep them from going to Europe but sometimes all the feeding and training is not going to work. I see rescue animals all the time that are unregistered, mentally abused as well as physically and totally unsuited for the weekend rider. One has to be sensible about what one can do about these animals.

If every person, who is intent on preserving every horse for whatever reason, would support two or more of them for ten to fifteen years, they would be more knowledgeable about the real cost of time and money involved in maintaining a horse. The population can only absorb so many horses, after that we must find something to do with the remainder.

My business and every other horseman's business depends on breeding, raising, training and selling foals by good stallions out of well-bred mares for a profit. If we can't do that, it becomes an expensive hobby. It is not, as many think, how many horses you own but the quality and breeding of the ones we have. We want to make money the same as everyone else but with the least cost. That does not mean that we cut corners to do that but we maintain the horses in a condition where they look good and are up-to-date on shots, farrier, etc.

I am constantly looking for mares with certain bloodlines to add to my program. It is not large but my mares are by the sons of leading sires or world champions out of the granddaughters of the same. My market is the person who is looking to buy a well-bred horse to start with. I price them to fit the pocketbook of that person. I sell a few babies a year and it adds to my enjoyment of life.

In my search, I come across mares that fit my requirements but have not produced what their potential is. In my opinion, they have not been crossed on the stallions they should have been. The owner may or may not thought of selling that mare. When I ask them if they want to sell, they immediately want more than the market. And these are the people with large numbers of mouths to feed and maintain. If they would have priced the mare according to the current market, I would probably have bought her even if she had never been vaccinated or wormed, or wasn't really well trained to ride. As long as there are not any unsoundness problems, I am confident in my ability to train the horse to do what I want. At some point in time, I would sell her but by adding value, i.e.; training or breeding to a really good stallion, I would make a profit.

On the other hand, I have seen people buy horses whose up-close breeding would indicate that they would be worth more as a gelding or riding horse than as a breeding animal. One must develop a sense of what is a potential breeding animal and what is better left as a riding or working horse. One can consult with the owners in their area who are selling animals about what bloodlines and conformation that are bringing prices that allow them to operate at a profit. Take their advice and start improving your programs.

In the spring of the year, we start thinking of advertising our stallion. You know the one in the barn who is a grandson of Super World Beater out of that Grand Old Mare. The one that is going to make us so much money we can retire.

There are articles appearing in every magazine telling us how to promote our stallion, how to choose the right stallion for our mares, and how to manage our stallion. I sometimes wonder how many of the writers actually make their living from breeding stallions to mares other than their own. I think that most have a day job just as the rest of us do.

If you were look up the facts on your particular breed, you would find that the majority of mares are bred to the more popular stallions; i.e. World Champions, Leading Sires, etc., while the majority of stallions were bred to five or less mares.

That fact should make you carefully consider whether your horse is truly stallion material. Has he done well enough in the show ring with others of his registry to be considered as a potential sire? Are his close-up relatives (sire and dam) of superior breeding and producers of individuals who are winners and close to the breed standard? Is his breeding something that mare owners would like to add to their programs?

Many of us tend to gloss over important information that should be used in making informed decisions. Human nature is to be the best at whatever we undertake to do. Therefore it is in our best interests to know the cost of the project—financially, personally, and socially before we jump in.

The equine lifestyle can be greatly rewarding. It can also

be devastating costly. In terms of relationships, one's mate can never understand why the horses consume so much of our time and dollars unless they too are in love with the animal. Our friends and relatives will question our wisdom about the amount of money spent on horses and related equipment.

When one decides to pursue a new hobby or business we should seek out people who can teach us what is involved in our new endeavors. Often times that is not the scenario when one decides to enter the horse world. We simply buy the first horse that fits our price range and then try to make it do what we want. This is true no matter what type of horse activity we enter; showing, breeding, endurance, etc. In breeding we buy the first mare that is priced to fit our pocketbook and breed her to the stallion what is also priced to fit our purse.

Everyone will tell you that they don't do that. However, if you take the time to pursue a few horse publications, you will find advertised the results of such undertakings. The ads will say that they have such and such well known bloodlines in their animals. Usually it is in the fourth or fifth generation. Close-up relatives are just another horse. The parents do not have a show record or progeny with a performance record.

In any other venue we would walk away from such odds against our winning. But, hope springs eternal. We will breed our mare or stallion to the first horse that catches our eye and heart. If we would take time to enlist the help of knowledge-able individuals in our pursuit of the perfect horse, we could save time, effort and money.

Everyone wants to have the best that they can afford. The horse industry is a multi-leveled sport where everyone can play. We should take time to learn the rules and how to play first. Then we should develop a game plan and follow it. If it needs revising, then we should do that as quickly as possible. If the horse you own is not going to accomplish what you want after you have given enough time and effort to his promotion, training, etc., then look for another who will allow you to reach your goals. We should review our goals in a timely manner and see if they are attainable. If not, then we should take those steps that will allow us to attain them.

Not every horse should be used as a stallion or as a broodmare. There will always be a greater market for well broke riding horses than for fire –breathing stallions or pregnant mares of nondescript breeding. On the other hand, people will flock to your door to breed to your champion. They will also give you a tremendous deal for the opportunity to breed your champion mare. The old adage 'Breed the Best to the Best to Get the Best' applies at all times.

25

Trainers and Training

One of my favorite remarks to an owner who is having a problem with their horse is, "You are better trainer than me." I am not being facetious or malicious. It is true. The owner spends more time with the horse than I. I get to work on him an hour or so a day for 30 to 90 days then he goes home. The owner does not think like I do and may not communicate with the animal like I do. That is not necessarily wrong but their influence is on a day by day basis while mine is short term.

Everyone can train an animal if they have patience and persistence and the willingness to be innovative in their approach. In other words, if what you are trying to get the horse to do isn't working, don't get mad but sit down and analyze the situation and try something different to reach the same result. I once bought a mare that had been pecked at by a person who was inexperienced and unwilling to try something new. I retrained the mare using different commands for everything. Once she learned those, it was easy to switch her back to the more conventional commands because she was more relaxed and receptive to what was asked of her.

In this time of everyone giving clinics on everything from groundwork to some of the very complicated events, every owner who wants to is getting a little bit of knowledge. They go right home and apply it to their own horse, which hasn't a clue to what is going on. The owner keeps pecking away at him and in the end both are mad and frustrated.

I wish that every owner had to spend a year or so with as many horses as possible. They are all different. How they were raised, the environment that they were kept in, how much handling they had from the very beginning affects how they react when we start to get serious about doing something with them. You can read books and attend clinics but in the end, the horse that you are working with is not the horse at the clinic or in the book. He is an individual with his own history and your job is to figure out how he can learn what you want and not be afraid or worried about what is going on.

One of the things that I encountered in my travels to different areas was they had a trainer who was well known in that area. And the question invariably was, "What do you think of so and so?" Of course, I had never heard of the person and didn't know what his credentials were or how good he was. There are a multitude of horse trainers who can ride a horse but there are very few that can get the horse to respond to them. Some trainers are good and some not so good. A good trainer takes time to watch the horse and his response to different stimuli. Just knowing what the probable reaction will be is extremely helpful. Some people create a scenario in their head based on their own previous experience and thinks that this particular horse or any horse for that matter fits that mold. Horses are individuals just as people are, what will work for one may not work for the next one. That is one reason why we have a lot of different bits, headstalls and other tack hanging in the tack room.

Any horse owner who comtemplates using a horse trainer to start or finish a horse, should do some research before committing their horse to them. Many trainers have the hired help start your horse as they have to concentrate on the few horses that really pay the bills. If you think that the trainer with many horses in his barn is riding and training every one, you have been mislead. There are only 24 hours in a day and if you are a busy barn, you may be able to get on 4 or 5 horses a day. That doesn't mean that you can follow through with what you want to do as the phone will ring or a client will stop by and you get interrupted. So, we have people, who want to be a trainer, work the horses and we are the man who collects the money. The person riding the horse may be a very competent horseman. He is paying his dues so one day he can be famous and renown.

You, as a horse owner, owe a responsibility to the animal to see that he is trained without gimmicks or obsolete methods. Horses are not the same as they were 40 or 50 years ago. In the most part, they do not run in a semi-wild state but are raised in a more enclosed area and are subjected to people on a regular basis. They are wormed, have their feet trimmed and are handled more often. Their temperament has changed somewhat because they are subject to more noises and things, they are less liable to react to certain stimuli. Their flight mechanism has been altered but they will still resort to their basic instincts when subjected to something new. It is the trainer's responsibility to desensitize them first and then develop their natural talents by humane methods. A trainer who is soft voiced and easy natured with a good set of hands, a natural balance in the saddle and is patient and persistent will accomplish more with a horse in a shorter time than one who uses gimmicks and fear to train the horse.

The current crop of horsemen uses a more humane method than we used to. You seldom see a horse that has a leg tied up while saddling, or a Running W put on them to teach them that they cannot run away. We teach them to accept the saddle with more patience than before. We ride them in a round pen or similar enclosure before we take them outside. In the old days, one would buck them out until they stopped bucking and take them out and ride them outside, often in the same day.

Having said all this, many of us have our horses boarded out or at a trainer's barn at one time or another because we do not have the facilities or the expertise to keep them at home. If we own a stallion or mares, we may send them out to be bred for the same reason.

We expect to get them back in the same or better shape than when they left. Sometimes, we don't. They are injured or crippled or worse. The question is how we, as owners, can minimize this.

When deciding where to board your horse or put him with a trainer, make a checklist. The list should include things like feed, stall, turnout time, blanketing, who to call in case of accident, insurance (what they have and what you should have) who takes care of the horse and references.

Take some time before you have to board the horse or send him out to the trainer to actually visit the facilities and the people involved. Look for things like stalls needing boards replaced, latches that don't work, unsafe fencing, and nails protruding in areas where horses are tied or kept. I have seen stallions kept in old chicken houses. They did not have the room to lift their heads or to move around comfortably.

If you are sending them to a trainer, talk to the trainer. Ask him about who is going to ride the horse (it may not be who you think). Watch the trainer in action aboard a client's horse.

Are they soft but firm? Or are they a little impatient and use gimmicks to accomplish their tasks?

Once you have decided on two or three prospective facilities or trainers ask to see their contracts (written, not verbal). Discuss with them each item in the contract. If you are uncomfortable or don't understand a paragraph, ask them to explain it. If you still don't understand it, ask for a copy and go see your legal advisor.

Contracts are sometimes pretty ambivalent. They are taken from a book, downloaded from the Net or written by someone other than an attorney. The language is very general and designed to cover 50 states. A good contract will have been drawn up by an attorney and be slanted in favor of the person that had it done. That is not bad but you, as the client should be aware of it. A prudent businessperson will not try to take advantage of his customers but on the other hand, they do not want to lose the farm over some incident that was not caused by their negligence.

There are a lot of horse businesses that post the Equine Limited Liability signs on their premises and is sure that they are protected from lawsuits. They are relying on the public's ignorance of what the law actually says. They assume since they had the client sign a release of liability when they came thru the door that they are not responsible for acts of negligence.

People think that if they don't have a written contract or insurance, they can't be sued or it is the horse owner's responsibility to insure his horse. If you say or do anything that the other party agrees to verbally or by their actions, you have made a commitment and have a contract to do what you said you would do. That includes returning the horse to the owner in the same or better condition than when you received the animal.

Owners have a responsibility to themselves and their horses

to insure the animal against mortality, injuries, colic, etc., particularly if the animal is valuable both monetarily and sentimentally. Horses get into trouble for no reason other than they are animals and certain instincts cause them to react to external stimuli.

Stable owners and trainers should have care, custody and control insurance plus commercial equine liability insurance. Commercial equine liability covers the business in case the Limited Equine Liability act fails.

Before you take your horse to a stable or trainer, ask if they have the above coverage. If they don't, do not put your horse with them. When something happens, an accident or injury, you want to know that you have some recourse to take care of the expenses.

If your barn takes on a trainer, you do not have to put your horse in training with that trainer. If your horse needs training or a tune-up, look around before making a decision on whom and where. Good trainers do not have to advertise or beg in order to get horses. (I never advertised that I was a trainer yet I had more horses to work than some that advertised.)

An owner should not assume that because the stable owner has insurance that the trainer has insurance also. You should check to see whose insurance covers your horse. If the stable owner is responsible for the feeding and care, then his CCC insurance should cover that and only that. The trainer should have Equine Liability to cover accidents that occur while he is riding or showing the horse. The stable owner or trainer cannot be held responsible for accidents that occur when one or the other is not in control of the animal.

Final word--It is the owner who has to assume the responsibility for where he stables or who trains the horse.

26

Foundation Horses

If Paint is a Quarter Horse with excessive white, what is a Quarter Horse? A Quarter Horse is a Thoroughbred outcross. A Thoroughbred is an Arabian outcross.

I often make those statements to clients who are impressed by bloodlines. It is my way of making them think about how many of today's breeds actually got started. We often forget or don't know how some of the breeds actually originated. To add to the confusion, we have associations that are reviving the foundation (?) bloodlines of their breed of choice.

When the Foundation Registries started up, I was amazed to learn that Poco Bueno was a foundation sire. I had thought that he was the great grandson of a foundation sire. The quarter horse breed traces back to twelve stallions that either were Thoroughbreds or sired by Thoroughbreds. They were bred to mares that were not as hot-blooded and so the disposition of the animal changed to a calmer, more even minded individual. In modern times, in order to increase the athletic ability of the quarter horse, breeders bred back to Thoroughbreds. These crosses have produced animals that excel in conformation, cutting, reining and as all around riding animals.

Considered by many Quarter Horse breeders to be the patriarch of the breed is an imported Thoroughbred, Janus (1680-1746). The modern day equivalent is another Thoroughbred, Three Bars, a sire of both Thoroughbreds and Quarter Horses. His progeny and their progeny dominate the show ring, cutting horse and the pleasure horse world.

Some of the leading Paint sires of our time were Quarter Horses. Painted Robin and Triples Titan are just two that come to mind. In today's registry, they could be registered as Quarter Horses but not in the Regular Paint registry. Why? They do not have one registered Paint parent. Painted Robin was by the Quarter Horse sire, Robin Boy by Robin Reed out of Midwest Snuffy (QH). Triples Titan was by Triple Image, a leading sire, out of the quarter mare, Sage.

Appaloosa breeders have the same background. Bright Eyes Brother, Hall of Fame sire is by a Quarter Horse, Billy Maddon, out of a Quarter Horse mare, Plaudette, who produced a Quarter Horse Champion Running Mare, Maddon's Bright Eyes. Plaudette was by a Thoroughbred, King Plaudit out of a Peter McCue mare.

Pinto horses have been around a long time and have come from many of the different breeds in vogue at the time. For a long time they were discriminated against by their registries. Pinto Arabians, Tennessee Walkers, Saddlebreds were at first unable to be registered by their respective registries and it took some breeders a very long time to accomplish being able to register their pinto offspring. Often these pintos came from bloodlines that were considered to be the foundation of the breed. There was a granddaughter of Flyhawk (a foundation Morgan sire) who was a chestnut overo and produced both colored and non-colored foals. The Arabian, Abu Farwa, produced a lot of white on his foals, enough that some produced pintos that couldn't be registered at the time. Tennessee Walkers have always had a lot of white and tended to produce pintos. The Spotted Saddle Horse Assn. was formed to register these pintos and give them an avenue to perform.

When the Thoroughbred was first being developed, they were the products of three Arabian stallions. You could not have a Thoroughbred without being able to trace back to one or more of those three stallions. The three were the Byerly Turk, the Godolphin Barb and the Darley Arabian. They were crossed on a number of Barb mares that were imported by King Charles.

The Byerly Turk's most prominent descendant was Herod. The horse, Matchem, was a grandson of the Barb and the Darley Arabian sired two great horses that went on to out produce themselves, Flying Childers and Barlett's Childers.

Up to 1940, the Arabian Registry was part of the American Studbook maintained by the American Jockey Club in this country. This brought up some interesting complexities in later years. Remember that a Thoroughbred produced some of the leading Quarter Horse stallions and mares. There was an Arabian stallion in Colorado who produced a number of Arabians, Quarter Horses and Thoroughbreds. He had an AHR number and a JC number and so his get were able to be registered in several registries depending on the mare's breed.

The Saddlebred as we know it now did not exist a century ago. The history of the breed starts in Virginia, Kentucky, Tennessee and Missouri. Much of the development was done in Kentucky and so they were known as 'Kentucky saddle horses'. Most of the earliest registered horses had some Thoroughbred blood crossed on trotting and slow pacing mares. Remember that all Thoroughbreds in the beginning had to trace to one of three Arabians. Rabiyas and Raseyn, Arabians, were five-gaited and exhibited as such at Kellogg Arabians.

Saddlebreds were able to walk, trot, canter and they were capable of racking, doing a running walk or fox trotting or slow pace. I bet you thought that only Tennessee Walkers did that. Those saddle horses that did the running walk are the foundation of today's Walking Horses.

One of the foundation sires for today's Standardbred was a Thoroughbred named Messenger. While he did not produce any trotters himself, his son Mambrino produced Abdallah a noted sire of trotters in America. Another sire of trotters was the stallion, Justin Morgan. Justin Morgan is recognized as the founding sire of the Morgan Horse. In some circles, he was thought to be descended from Thoroughbred breeding.

Today's foundation breeders are for the most part trying to revert to the past when the horse was used for a variety of jobs. He pulled the plow or delivery wagon all week and on Sundays was the family buggy horse or was at the bush track running against other horses.

The breed registries are starting to realize that most of the horses, people own in today's world, do a multitude of tasks. They are used to work cattle, teach the kids how to ride, barrel race for Mom and rope for Dad and still look good enough to show at halter in the morning and do performance events in the afternoon. The AQHA has recognized this and is starting to promote performance halter classes.

In the market, these horses are still bringing decent prices as compared to the one-event horses where the demand has dropped dramatically. I monitor several sales across the nation and have watched what used to be really hot breeding, sired by leading sires, bring less than the stud fee. If you have training and upkeep added in, you really have a loss that the IRS is going to question at some time about your profit motive if you have one.

As one person put it, you need to get rid of ones that you are just feeding and buy one or two really good ones. If you are breeding because you have mares and a stallion and are selling the results for canner prices, you may want to change your program completely. From a business standpoint, and the IRS's, that will make more sense than holding on to what you have and trying to make a profit. I have heard all the stories about how the public does not know a good horse when they see one but who else is going to buy the horse. That applies to those horses that are foundation breeding (?) as well as the ones that are not.

When something first gets hot, lots of us get lucky and do really well at first. Then the market becomes more educated and shifts to a more realistic view of things and everything shifts back to normal. At that time, if you have been watching and listening to the buying public, you will have upgraded your program and still be able to break even. I don't have a problem with foundation breeding because at one time or another in my life with horses, I have bred, trained or sold horses that are considered foundation in today's world. But as the market shifted, I had a choice, either to make a living or to find new employment.

If you are profit motivated, you will continually be looking for ways to improve your profit margins. If you are a hobbyist, you may not care at first but at some time you will want sell or trade your horse(s) for a different one. One always wants to recoup some of the investment that you have put in the horse and the only way to do that is to have something the public wants to buy.

27

Reminisce

Finally I want to share a few observations with you. This year (2013) I have been involved professionally with horses and the horse industry for 58 years. Actually, I was raised around horses and cows. My father and grandfather farmed with horses until the 1960's. They had work horses that pulled the plow, the mower and rake, stacked the hay and logged the timber. The saddle horses were not of any particular breed but decent animals who knew how to chase cows, rope stock for doctoring and branding, just good ranch horses.

I have seen the horse industry evolve from the horse being used as a work animal whose job was to help you, the human, get the work done to the present time where he is a companion who helps his master to enjoy life and his surroundings.

During my childhood days, good using horses could be purchased for $25-100. Wild horses were rounded up in large numbers and marketed. The good ones found employment; the rest went to Europe. The good ones were used in everyday ranch or farm life and the mares were bred to good local studs to produce the next crop. We did not give a hoot whether they had papers or not. A good horse was a good horse.

In this time, when we have foundation registries, color registries, breed registries and so on and so on, I wonder if any of you know what the horse of fifty years ago looked like or did. In the beginning we had saddle horses and/or work horses. The saddle horses were of Thoroughbred ancestry or could trace back to that breed. The work horses were heavy draft breeds or draft breed crosses that stood 16 hands or better. They were expected to work 14-hour days. There were not any stalls, unless you had lots of money. There were tie stalls and corrals. Period. Feed was grain and pasture in summer and hay in the winter. The horses that were kept up in the winter to feed the cows were given grain but they were the only ones.

Probably one of the reasons that when I retired, I moved to Missouri. I live in the midst of Amish and Mennonite country where the horse is still a work animal. They pull the family buggy and work cattle as they did when I was growing up. There are areas in America where the culture is still much the same as it was before WWII. When people have a party, it is often a trail ride through the country side with a potluck supper afterwards. Much like yesteryear, during harvest time, when everyone helped each other to harvest the crops. At the center of it all is the horse and it's owner.

When I went to college, I was exposed to the world of horse shows and livestock exhibitions. Up to that time, I was a ranch kid in a small town in Southwestern Idaho. I found that people did more with the horse than chase cows or use them in rodeos.

The first horse I worked with knew more than I. A classmate of mine was injured and needed someone to tune her horse for the rodeo season. The girl was a can chaser and the horse was really good at his job. Suffice to say I learned a lot about barrel horses and I still have sore knees.

Between semesters at college, I worked at Boeing Aircraft in Seattle. I found out I would rather be working with animals than building 707's. I hung out at the area stables, eventually riding and training horses for clients.

In 1959, I opened my own barn in the area and from there on I never was without a horse to ride. I trained whatever the client brought; Arabians, Quarter Horses, Morgans, Saddlebreds, Galienco, POA's, etc. In those days, you showed the same horse in halter and riding classes, both English and Western. You might even use him in the hunter and jumper classes.

Much of that type of competition is gone now as many of your conformation horses can't ride worth a darn and vice-versa. I believe that horses can look pretty and still be comfortable to ride without falling apart. But that is my opinion and what I look for in a horse when I am buying. And when I sell it my market is a lot broader than before. Today's riders are often recreational riders who are looking for a well-broke horse that can do many things. The horse does not have to excel at everything or anything but should be willing to do what is asked of it.

Along the way, I noticed I had a lot of income and a lot more outgo. That is when I returned to college to get the business degree. One of my better decisions. I learned marketing; accounting procedures; business law and whole lot more.

I changed the way I did things. Now I get a P & L statement each month so I can spot trouble before it costs me a lot of money. I marketed my services to a broader range of clientele and I was able to increase my gross profit and my net profit as well. I went from having a day job to support my horse habit to having my horse habit support my family and me.

You don't have to be world famous to make a living at horses. You do have to have dedication and ambition. Any business owner needs to have those qualities if his business is to succeed. You want to have a service or product that is needed and in demand in your market area. One of the lessons, I have learned over the years is that you have to stand on the same street corner. If you do, you will see more people than if you change corners every time something goes wrong or life changes. People get to recognize you and your product or service and your business will prosper. You will learn to be innovative in your marketing and to upgrade your service on a regular basis. You will listen to your clients and strive to fill their wants as your business progresses. By doing so, your business should prosper and thrive and you will be more content with your work.

Be patient. Endure the bad times as well as the good. Do the best you can for everyone, whether you believe the horse or client is good or bad. Be honest. If you don't believe the horse can do what the client wants it to do, tell them without prejudice. Just because the person down the street has told them different, that does not mean you are wrong.

Above all, enjoy life. Wake up each morning with an eager attitude to do the best you can. Smile often, don't get too serious about the events of everyday living. Love your significant other, your children, your friends and enemies. Be tolerant of all people and things. Most of all; be happy and content with you.

Biography

M. R. Bain was born in a small southwestern Idaho town that was settled by his great grandparents. He grew up with cows, horses and other farm animals. Early on, he determined that he wanted to be involved with horses as his grandparents and parents had been. To that end, he has devoted his life to horses and their owners.

He has been successfully involved the horse industry since 1955. While in college, he had the opportunity to work for and with some of the top owners and trainers of that time. Upon graduating with a degree in Animal Husbandry, he opened his own training stable in the Seattle, WA area in 1959. He brought some of the first POA ponies to that area in 1960, importing them from Mexico for the owners. He returned to college in 1963 to get a degree in Business Administration.

He has bred, trained and shown Quarter Horses, Appaloosas, Paints, Arabians as well as Morgans, Saddlebreds, Welsh Ponies and many other breeds. He has developed breeding programs and farms for owners, managed boarding and training stables, been a stallion manager and is considered an authority on equine business management.

He is a published writer and lecturer on the horse industry. His articles have appeared in The Quarter Horse Journal,
Paint Horse Journal, Pinto Horse Magazine, POA Magazine,
Spotted Saddle Horse News and 30 regional horse publications
from Florida to Alaska and East to West Coast since 1994.

Upon retiring from active training and showing in 2001,
he has devoted his energies to teaching others about the business aspects of the industry with his articles and clinics on 'The
Business of Horses'. This book is based on his own experience
in the horse industry and the result of those articles and clinics.

CPSIA information can be obtained at www.ICGtesting.com
Printed in the USA
LVOW07s2056210415

435488LV00001B/101/P

9 781478 721987